A PREDATOR WITHIN

A Family Playbook for Prevention and Restoration

Angela Rodgers

Battle Press
SATELLITE BEACH, FLORIDA

A Predator Within: A Family Playbook for Prevention and Restoration

A Predator Within may be ordered through booksellers or by contacting:

www.Angelamrodgers.com

contact@angelamrodgers.com

ISBN: (SC) 979-8-9988646-6-7
ISBN: (eBook) 979-8-9988646-3-6

Printed in the United States of America.

First Edition.

Table Of Contents

ALSO BY ANGELA RODGERS

PAINFULLY BROKEN YET BEAUTIFULLY REDEEMED

FROM DARKNESS TO LIGHT

Dedication:

For the parents who pick up this book—those who are tired, afraid, furious, and fiercely determined—this is for you. Keep doing the brave work; your vigilance changes everything.

About the Author

Angela Rodgers is unapologetically a lover and teacher of Christ. This relationship was fortified even greater as God restored her through the deaths of her two sons. As the founder of Millstone Ministry, she is a national educator on human trafficking, online exploitation, and digital safety. For more than a decade, she has worked on the front lines— partnering with law enforcement, child-advocacy centers, and survivor services—to rescue and restore victims and to equip communities to prevent harm.

Angela is a fierce advocate for children, and this type of advocacy is only birthed out of true adversity. She is not afraid to share the raw and personal details of her tragedies and grief in order to help others understand the redeeming and healing love of God.

But equally important, she and her husband, Myke, have opened their home to more than 200 foster children and have adopted eleven. She travels the U.S. delivering trauma-informed training for churches, schools, and community organizations and leads practical street-outreach and survivor-support efforts through Millstone Ministry.

Angela lives in Michigan with her family, grandchildren, and dogs, and brings together faith, lived experience, and evidence-based practice to protect children and strengthen communities.

Preface

How to Use this Book

This book was written to be used, not merely read. Treat it as a toolkit you keep within arm's reach—a manual for urgent moments, a training program for daily life, and a blueprint for long-term cultural change in your home, church, school, or community. Inside you'll find two complementary strands on every major topic: vetted, professional recommendations that reflect best practices from the field followed by our real-world, family-tested approach that shows how those recommendations can be lived out in a high-trauma household. Read both. The professionals give you the "why" and the evidence; the family sections give you the "how" and the practical adjustments that make protection possible day to day.

If you need one thing right now, use the Quick-Action resources up front: emergency scripts, immediate response checklists, and evidence-preservation steps. Put those pages where you can reach them in a crisis—on the fridge, in your phone, and in every caregiver's glovebox. If a child is in immediate danger, do not hesitate to call emergency services first. This book supplements action; it does not replace police, child protective services, or medical care.

For steady progress, read the book in two passes. First, bookmark and skim the Practical Resources and the chapters on emergency response, digital threats (AI, sexting, sextortion), and device lockdown—these are the highest-risk areas where quick changes save lives. Second, work through the book chapter by chapter, implementing the checklists, practicing the role-play scripts with your children, and adapting the family models to your household. Use the printable templates to codify rules, set a family code word, and build a safety binder that includes contact numbers, evidence preservation instructions, and the names of local advocates and hotlines.

Make it collaborative. This is not a solo project for one parent. Share key sections with co-parents, grandparents, babysitters, youth leaders, teachers, and trusted neighbors. Hold an initial "family safety summit" using the conversation scripts in the Practical Resources: set clear, consistent boundaries together; agree on device rules; assign who will be the emergency contact; and commit to regular check-ins. When institutions—schools, churches, or clubs—are involved, bring the relevant chapter to leaders and ask for written policies, background-check confirmation, and a visible two-adult rule for youth activities.

Practice more than policy. Rules alone won't protect a child unless they're rehearsed until they become reflex. Use the role-play scripts, safety words, and short scenario drills regularly and casually—on car rides, after dinner, or before sleepovers—so responses feel automatic to your children. Teach anatomical language and consent scripts early, and model calm, non-punitive responses when a child discloses. If a disclosure happens, follow the emergency and evidence-preservation steps precisely and reach out to trained advocates immediately.

Adapt with discernment. Every family, culture, and community is different. Use the professional guidance as baseline standards and the family examples as potential adjustments—not rigid rules you must copy exactly. If your household faces specific vulnerabilities—trauma history, foster care, homelessness, or mental-health challenges— prioritize the chapters on trauma, mental-health vulnerability, and human trafficking, and enlist local professionals to create a tailored safety plan.

Take care of yourself. Protecting children is emotionally demanding work. Use the short sections on self-care and debriefing: name your limits, organize backup caregivers, and join a peer support group or professional supervision if you're working with survivors. You cannot protect well from a place of exhaustion, shame, or silence— seek help and let others carry the load with you.

Finally, this book is an invitation to act, not to hide in fear. Let it sharpen your vigilance, expand your language, and arm you with simple, repeatable practices that reduce risk and restore safety. Keep the printables where you can use them. Revisit this guide annually and whenever technology, tactics, or circumstances change. And above all, believe that steady, ordinary acts of care—clear boundaries, honest conversation, and timely action—are the most powerful defenses we have.

Disclaimer

The information in this book is provided for education and awareness only. It is not a substitute for legal, medical, mental-health, or other professional advice tailored to your specific situation. Laws, policies, and recommended practices vary by jurisdiction and change over time; do not rely on this book alone to make decisions that could affect a child's safety or legal rights. If a child is in immediate danger, call local emergency services right away. If you suspect abuse, exploitation, or trafficking, contact law enforcement, child protective services, or a qualified local advocate without delay.

Neither the author nor the publisher assumes liability for actions taken—or not taken—based on the material in this book. Practical guidance, examples, and personal stories are intended to illustrate common risks and safety strategies; they are not case-specific counsel. Before initiating legal action, confronting an accused person, or implementing major interventions, consult attorneys, trained social-service professionals, or medical and mental-health experts to protect the child and preserve the integrity of any investigation.

Mandatory reporting duties differ by state and by role. If you are unsure of your responsibilities, contact your local child-protective agency, an attorney, or your professional licensing board. This is a work of creative nonfiction. While all the stories in this book are true, all names and identifying details have been changed to protect the privacy of the people involved.

Some names and identifying details have been changed to protect the privacy of individuals. Any similarities to persons, living or deceased, are purely coincidental and unintentional.

Chapter 1

How this Book Works and Why It Matters

R ead this book and do the work. You will find life-saving pages—emergency scripts, immediate response checklists, and evidence-preservation steps.

Next, move through the book with purpose, not passivity. Implement the checklists, set the household rules, and rehearse the short scripts with your children until they are automatic. Make small changes tonight—one rule, one code word, one tech setting—and build from there. Run short drills (five minutes) every week and a fuller review each month so safety becomes habit, not a someday idea.

You'll notice some steps repeat across chapters. That's deliberate. I want a parent to be able to open to a chapter that is relevant and have all the steps listed there without having to search. The same core actions—clear language, immediate reporting, removing access, preserving evidence, and steady adult response—apply whether the risk shows up online, at a sleepover, in a youth group, or at home. Repetition is how these responses become muscle memory in moments that matter.

Don't wait for perfect conditions. Share these pages with co-parents, babysitters, youth leaders, and trusted friends. Teach one caregiver tonight what to do and then teach another. This book is designed to be used in pieces and repeated until protection feels natural. Act now—small, consistent steps save children.

CHAPTER NOTES:

Chapter 2

"Stranger" Danger Redefined

Every time I speak—in schools, churches, agencies, or community groups—one question always comes: *How do we protect our children when predators hide right where we live, work, and play?*

I've heard it from parents, professionals, and even children themselves. Their fear is the reason I wrote this book.

These pages will not be easy. Some truths cut too close to home. Before, you might have said, "I didn't know this could happen." After this, you will never be able to say that again. My goal is not to terrify you but to wake you up—to move us from ignorance to awareness, and from awareness to action.

I am not offering a polished manual with neat answers. What follows is my testimony—drawn from decades of working with foster children, and from valleys of loss I have walked myself. These stories carry scars. But silence has never saved a child. Truth, no matter how heavy, can.

When Danger Was Simple

Growing up, danger felt easier to recognize. It lived outside. We were told not to talk to strangers, not to climb into cars, and to come home when the streetlights blinked on. I still hear my dad's whistle from the porch calling us home.

Life wasn't perfect, but it felt predictable. Strangers were "out there." We were "safe" in here. Phones were fixed to the wall, and "blocking" someone meant leaving the receiver off the hook so the line stayed busy. You could tell where the kids were by the amount of bikes laying in the yard.

We played outside from sunrise to sunset, carefree and unafraid, our days measured by laughter, not fear.

But that world is gone. Today, danger isn't waiting at the corner. It slips in quietly—through glowing screens, online games, and people we trust. Predators don't just wear ski masks. They wear usernames. They wear smiles we know.

Why I Won't Stay Silent

I know the cost of danger all too well. I buried two of my children.

In 2012, Jacob was taken from me in a double murder-suicide. Years later in 2017, Jarred died from an accidental gunshot wound after long struggles with mental health. These are words no mother should ever have to write.

I told their story in *Painfully Broken Yet Beautifully Redeemed*. But even now, every morning I wake up to their absence as sharp as the day I lost them. Their deaths carved a permanent ache in me—but also a permanent resolve: I will not stop sounding the alarm.

Fear Freezes. Love Moves.

That resolve is why I write, and why I speak. Not to paralyze you, but to move you. Fear freezes us, but love pushes us forward. Protecting children today requires more than warnings about strangers. It requires building nets of trust, vigilance, and communication—strong enough to catch them when danger comes.

This begins with conversations. Not lectures—conversations. Honest, ongoing talks that allow kids to speak. It means noticing quiet shifts: withdrawal, secrecy, silence. Silence often screams the loudest.

And we, as parents, must keep learning. We cannot shrug off the apps they use or the games they play. Asking questions is not prying—it's protecting. Boundaries are not control—they are meant for protection. Teach your children to listen to that gut feeling that whispers, "Something's not right." And make sure they know they can always come to you.

Strangers at the Table

For years, we taught "stranger danger." Don't take candy. Don't get in strange cars. But here is the truth: most children aren't harmed by strangers. We no longer live in the days of the "white creeper vans" we hear our children talk about. Its much worse and it is everywhere.

We have welcomed more than 200 foster children into our home. Not one was hurt by someone they didn't know. Every single child was harmed by someone they trusted—a parent, a relative, a neighbor, a coach, or someone online pretending to be a peer.

Strangers do not just lurk outside. They sit at our kitchen tables. They slip in through video games, music, movies, and social media. They do not look dangerous. They look normal. Fun. Safe.

But anything—or anyone—that cracks your child's trust, identity, or safety is a stranger. And that stranger is dangerous.

The Hardest Truth

This is the hardest truth to face: the people who hurt children most are rarely strangers. They are the ones we trust.

- The stepdad who tucks them in.
- The uncle who insists on "special" time.
- The coach who earns admiration, then exploits it.
- The babysitter no one questions.
- The youth leader who preaches purity but demands secrecy.
- Sometimes a parent.
- Sometimes a sibling.
- Often a friend, or a friend's sibling.

This is why so many children stay silent. How do you tell your mom that her boyfriend—the man she loves—is hurting you? How do you tell your dad his best friend crossed a line?

We need to stop lying to ourselves. Danger does not always wear a mask. Sometimes it wears a wedding ring. Sometimes it leads worship. Sometimes it is laughing with us at the barbecue or is invited to our kitchen table to break bread.

We cannot afford to dismiss red flags—adults who demand secrecy, isolate children, blur boundaries, or give inappropriate gifts or touch. These are not quirks. They are warnings. If we ignore them because they make us uncomfortable, we are choosing our comfort over our child's safety.

Knowledge Is Power

Yes, this reality is heavy. But fear will not protect our children—awareness will.

Build homes where children know they can speak freely. Notice changes in behavior. Teach them to trust their instincts. And when they confess mistakes, listen with empathy. If they can trust you with their failures, they'll trust you with their fears.

Protecting kids does not mean shielding them from every risk. It means equipping them to stand when risk finds them.

Redefining Stranger Danger

The old version doesn't fit anymore. Stranger danger is not just the man or woman in the parking lot. It is the voices we let into our homes, the screens we hand our children, and sometimes the people closest to us.

But this isn't only about danger—it's about resolve. Awareness builds strength. Awareness gives kids the courage to ask questions, speak up, and make wise choices.

Our job is not to hover in fear. It is to stay engaged—knowing who their friends are, monitoring online worlds, setting boundaries, and paying attention when something feels off. If we don't, someone else will. And too often, that "someone" is not safe.

So let us replace fear with vigilance. Silence with honesty. Naivety with wisdom.

Let's redefine stranger danger—not as a phrase that makes us tremble, but as a call to act with courage, vigilance, and love.

At the end of the day, this isn't just a fight against danger—it's a fight for our children's futures. We cannot wrap them in bubble wrap, but we can wrap them in faith, love, truth, and courage. We can raise them to recognize lies, to speak when silence feels safer, and to trust that the people who love them will listen. That is our power. That is our calling. And when awareness turns into action, when vigilance is fueled by love, we don't just guard their childhood—we help secure their tomorrow.

CHAPTER NOTES:

Chapter 3

Understanding Today's Risk

The world our children live in isn't just bigger than the one we grew up in—it's more dangerous, because it has no boundaries. Screens and social networks have demolished the walls that once separated home, school, and neighborhood. Predators no longer wait on the far side of town. They sit in your child's pocket, move at the speed of Wi-Fi, and wear the face of a "friend."

And here's the brutal truth: if you don't set boundaries inside your home, the world will set them for your child—and it will set them with cruelty. Without clear lines—what is safe, what is not, what is private, what must be shared—kids are left defenseless in a world built to exploit them. Home must be the training ground for boundaries, or the world will gladly deliver harsher lessons.

The dangers our kids face today didn't exist when we were young. One humiliating photo can reach thousands in seconds. One fake profile can deceive even the smartest teen. Apps with disappearing messages, encrypted chats, and hidden gaming servers create digital back alleys where predators thrive. This is the reality: the "playground" our children live in can turn into a trap without warning.

And the biggest threat isn't strangers—it's people your child already knows. Relatives. Coaches. Neighbors. Older peers. Predators don't storm in with threats. They slide in with trust. A little extra attention. A gift. A secret. Bit by bit, boundaries erode until loyalty is twisted into chains. By then, the child isn't just trapped—they're protecting the very person who is harming them. This is why children rarely "just tell." Fear. Shame. Loyalty. Silence.

Online, the attacks multiply. Predators pose as peers to flatter, isolate, and manipulate. Cyberbullying stalks children into their bedrooms. Peer-to-peer harm—sextortion, sexual pressure, coercion, and mob-style bullying—is destroying lives. The fallout is brutal: anxiety, depression, plummeting grades, and too often, suicide.

Environments either protect or endanger. A church that skips background checks, a coach alone with kids, a program that discourages questions—all of these create wide-open doors for predators. Institutions don't have to be evil to be unsafe. They only have to be careless.

The grooming pattern is always the same: access, attention, secrecy, isolation. The warning signs are there—if we have the courage to see them. A child suddenly becomes defensive about time spent with someone. Unexplained gifts. Withdrawal. Age-inappropriate knowledge. An adult who always asks for exceptions. One red flag may not prove anything. But patterns? Patterns scream.

So, what can parents do? Everything. Teach your kids the language of boundaries: "Stop." "That's private." "I don't like that." Practice scripts until they come naturally. Build a family code word for emergencies. Demand visibility—two adults present, no secrets, no unexplained gifts. Vet every caregiver, coach, and leader. Set tech rules, learn the apps, and normalize judgment-free conversations. And above all, believe them. The moment they speak up is the most important moment of their lives—and your reaction determines whether they'll ever speak again.

If you suspect harm, act. Remove the child. Save the evidence. Call professionals—child protective services, law enforcement, or a child advocacy center. Do not confront the abuser yourself. That puts your child at greater risk and destroys cases. Always err on the side of reporting. Silence protects predators. Reporting protects children.

Communities have a choice: protect children or protect predators. Churches, schools, and sports teams must enforce two-adult rules, background checks, real training, and cultures where questions are welcomed. Whistleblowers and victims must be supported, not shamed. Institutions are safest when transparency matters more than loyalty to leaders.

Parents, the deadliest lie you can believe is "It won't happen to us." That lie leaves your child unprotected. Predators don't care about your zip code, your values, or how fiercely you love your kids. They only care about opportunity. And the only defense is awareness backed by action.

Awareness without action is worthless. Talk about boundaries. Practice scripts. Vet environments. Demand accountability. Protecting your children doesn't mean distrusting everyone; it means refusing blind trust. Be the parent who listens. Be the adult your child knows will believe them. Because in the end, belief without action changes nothing. Belief with action saves lives.

CHAPTER NOTES:

Chapter 4

Building Open Communication

Put down your phone. Stop multitasking. Look your child in the eye. Or risk losing them. Guess what, I fail at this daily also. We all do when we hear "MOM" "MOM" "MOM" for the billionth time in a day. Oftentimes, tuning it out seems easier.

Right now, your child is deciding if you are safe to talk to—not tomorrow, not when life slows down. Today. Every time you cut them off, say "not now," or scroll while they're speaking, you send one message: silence is safer. Once they believe that, you don't get another chance. They won't stop talking altogether; they'll just stop talking to you.

Parenthood does not automatically earn trust. Trust is built, and it's built daily—by showing up, listening, and keeping your word. Break it once, they remember. Break it twice, and they shut down. If they can't trust you with the little things, they'll never trust bringing you the big things.

And one day, the big things will come. Abuse. Bullying. Drugs. Sex. Self-harm. That moment will arrive. If you've practiced listening, they'll keep talking. If not, they'll decide silence is safer.

Don't wait for "the big talk." Communication doesn't thrive in staged, once-in-a-while conversations. It grows in the cracks—on the ride to practice, at the dinner table, in the whispered bedtime story. Those are the doorways. Miss enough of them, and the door slams shut. And once it's shut, it doesn't open easily.

Safety talks aren't optional. The world is already speaking to your child—strangers online, classmates in the hallways, peers at parties. If you don't speak, the world will. And the world doesn't care if your child survives it. You do. So don't terrify them into silence, but don't leave them unprepared. Teach them: *"You can say no." "You can walk away." "You can tell me anything."* If you don't, someone else will teach them their voice doesn't matter.

And remember this: you are their mirror. If you bury your feelings, they'll bury theirs. If you explode, they'll explode. If you shut down, they'll shut down. Every time you brush off your emotions with "I'm fine," you're teaching them to hide theirs. But every time you admit, "I'm struggling, and here's how I'm handling it," you're teaching them courage. So, check your own "mirror" first.

When your child risks telling you something real, you get one chance. Panic, and you'll scare them. Judge, and you'll drive them into secrecy. Preach, and you'll shut them down. In those fragile moments, your response decides if they'll ever risk that kind of honesty again.

Picture this: your child is being groomed online but stays silent because they know you'll explode. Or they're bullied daily, but don't tell you because you minimize their pain. Maybe they're sneaking alcohol or pills to cope, but your anger feels scarier than their addiction. Or the nightmare—your "quiet" kid, the one you thought was "just private," is secretly cutting themselves, or planning not to be here tomorrow. You'll swear you had no idea. But silence doesn't come from nowhere. It's trained—one missed moment at a time.

Silence should terrify you. Stop saying, "My kid just isn't a talker." No. Silence is not a personality trait. Silence is a wall. Silence is fear. Silence is a smoke alarm you're ignoring because you don't see flames—yet.

I'll be honest: I fail at this daily. I hear "Mom" a hundred times an hour. I get dismissive. I half-listen. I nod without really hearing. And then a bigger problem explodes because I ignored the smaller ones. That's the cost of not listening. The little moments always grow into big ones. I'm in this fight with you—failing, and trying again, every single day.

Here's the truth: open communication is not optional. It is survival. It is the difference between being your child's safe harbor and being the storm they avoid. If you're not building trust, you're breaking it. If you're not listening, you're teaching them to hide. If you're not their safe place, someone else will be. You need to make sure that someone is you.

Call to Action

Stop making excuses. Stop hoping they'll "grow out of it." Stop pretending silence is harmless. Start listening. Train yourself to pause, look them in the eye, and hear even the "small" things. Because the small things are how you earn the right to the big ones.

The question isn't, *"Will my child talk?"* The question is, *"Who will they talk to?"* And you need to make sure the answer is you.

When you're getting irritated and tuning out MOM, MOM, DAD, DAD for the millionth time, remember I have two children who I would give anything to hear those words from again. This is something I personally continue to work on.

CHAPTER NOTES:

Chapter 5

Digital Weapons

Would you ever hand your child a loaded gun and say, *"Figure it out?"* Would you pass them a running chainsaw and walk away? I would hope that no parent would. Yet every day, well-meaning parents hand their children smartphones, tablets, and gaming consoles with barely a word of caution. The truth is that these devices are more dangerous than a gun or a chainsaw. Guns wound the body. Phones and gaming can wound the soul.

If you wouldn't leave your child alone at Disney, don't leave them alone online. Disney sees around 35,000 visitors a day, and most parents would never allow their child to wander there unsupervised because there are too many strangers and too many unknowns. Yet online, there are over 500,000 predators actively seeking to connect with children every single day.

The internet is the largest crowd your child will ever be in, but it is invisible to you. If a crowded theme park makes you cautious, the online world should make you even more alert. Your child is not "just online." They are in a space filled with strangers, risks, and people who are intentionally looking for them. Your child holds the access to the darkest corners of the internet in the palm of their hand — pornography, predators, traffickers, cyberbullies, scammers, and content engineered to addict their developing brains. Unlike a cut or bruise you can see, the wounds from digital danger bleed silently: shame, secrecy, addiction, depression, self-harm. By the time parents notice, the damage is often deep.

Here's what's at stake:

- **Pornography** that rewires the brain and distorts healthy relationships.
- **Predators and traffickers** who patiently groom children online, posing as friends until trust is built and boundaries collapse.
- **Cyberbullying and harassment** that follow kids 24/7, not just on the playground.
- **Permanent digital footprints**—a careless photo, a screen shot of a private message, a search history leaked that can resurface years later to destroy reputations, relationships, and opportunities.
- **Apps and games designed for addiction,** built to keep kids scrolling, clicking, and spending.

Think your child is too young or too smart to be targeted? Think again. Predators and algorithms don't discriminate. They go where the kids are. The moment your child logs in, he or she is a target.

This is why digital parenting cannot be passive. Filters and restrictions are not optional; they're seat belts. Think of it this way. If you need milk you go to the grocery store. If you need gas in your car you go to a gas station. Where do you think predators look for kids - where they hang out which is online.

But seat belts alone won't keep your kids safe on the digital highway—you also have to teach them how to drive: when to brake, how to navigate, and what to do when danger appears.

Start with crystal-clear boundaries:

- **Device-free zones:** no phones in bedrooms, bathrooms, no screens at the dinner table.
- **Time limits:** define usage hours and enforce downtime.
- **Approved apps only:** nothing new without parental review.

Then use the tools available. Monitoring isn't spying—it's protecting. Apps like **Bark** scan texts, emails, and more than 30 platforms for signs of cyberbullying, sexting, suicidal thoughts, grooming, or explicit content, and send you alerts. **Covenant Eyes** monitors screen activity and sends accountability reports to trusted adults, helping safeguard against pornography and hidden browsing. These aren't luxuries; they're lifelines. If you wouldn't let your child drive without a seatbelt, why let them scroll without protection?

But tools aren't enough. The most powerful safeguard is your voice. Have relentless conversations about why rules exist. Teach your children to recognize grooming tactics—secrecy, flattery, requests for personal photos, attempts to move conversations off-platform. Roleplay their responses: *"Block. Screenshot. Tell me."* Normalize the idea that coming to you—even with mistakes—won't bring punishment but protection.

Don't underestimate digital permanence. Make sure your child knows the internet never forgets, teach them that it is Public and Permanent. A photo sent in trust can be weaponized in shame. A cruel comment posted in anger can live forever. Walk through their settings with them. Show them how to disable location sharing, set strong passwords, and enable two-factor authentication. Audit their digital footprint together and talk about what you find.

The stakes couldn't be higher. You wouldn't ignore smoke in your child's room, yet too many parents ignore the glowing screen in their hand until it's too late. Your child doesn't just need boundaries. They need your protection, your guidance, and your presence.

The digital world is not safe by default. You have to make it safe. And if you don't, someone else—with darker intentions—will.

Our Social Media Policy

I'll get pushback on this. That's fine. I'll say it plainly: **none of my minor children have social media.** Not because I want control, but because the other side of those screens is life-threateningly dangerous.

Behind a username, anyone can be anything. That anonymity isn't harmless—it's a predator's playground. Human trafficking, sexual exploitation, grooming, sextortion, pornography: these aren't distant headlines. They are organized harms, and they almost always begin online.

Studies show the vast majority of child sex crimes start with online contact. Why? Because the internet lets abusers lower a child's defenses invisibly, slowly, and with devastating precision. Also, you can be anyone you want online.

We live in a world where children as young as three have online profiles. Parents hand a tablet to a toddler to buy ten minutes of quiet, unaware of what lies beyond the screen. Victims have been groomed on "G-rated" apps and games— places parents assume are safe. Those aren't isolated cases. They're warnings.

The risks are constant. Platforms collect names, locations, contact lists, browsing habits—data that can be mined, sold, and weaponized. A photo meant for Grandma can be repurposed, shared, and used against a child for years.

Location tags and live updates create a real-time map of their lives. Children rarely grasp permanence; they can't imagine how one careless post could shadow them for decades.

The mental health toll is brutal. Social media compresses a child's world into highlight reels they can't compete with. Constant comparison breeds shame, anxiety, and depression. Cyberbullying is relentless when tormentors are just a tap away at any hour. Algorithms engineered for engagement hook attention, fracture sleep, shorten focus, and prime kids for addictive behaviors—at the expense of learning, self-worth, and emotional stability.

Even the content itself is dangerous. Violent, sexual, and age-inappropriate material often slips past moderation. Misinformation spreads unchecked. Commercial pressures flood online feeds designed for gullible minds by normalizing risky behavior. Parental controls exist but are inconsistent, easily bypassed, and unreliable. Parents are left piecing together tools, vigilance, and education—none of which are foolproof.

This isn't scaremongering. It's reality. That's why we made a hard rule in our home: **no social media until graduation.** Harsh? Yes. Necessary? Absolutely. I expect arguments about autonomy. But I also know what's waiting behind the screen, how easily a child can be swayed, and how permanent the consequences can be.

We owe our children more than convenience. We owe them protection, presence, and time to grow without being monetized, groomed, or manipulated. This isn't about fear—it's about fierce, deliberate care.

Cell Phones, Electronics, and Gaming

We enforce a strict policy in our home because with many children under one roof—and the risks some of their biological parents could bring—we cannot leave

21

exposure to chance. Phones are introduced deliberately and gradually. Around age fourteen, they may earn use of a **Gabb phone** with calls, texts, music, and a few parent-approved apps—but no internet.

When they start driving, they may graduate to a full smartphone so we can monitor location, but social media remains off-limits. We allow only carefully chosen apps—YouTube for music, a Bible app, and, in one case, our daughter used Pinterest for crafting—with clear rules and oversight.

Every device runs **Bark**, which sets automated boundaries and alerts us to suspicious activity so we can step in early. **Covenant Eyes** reports inappropriate images or searches directly to us as accountability partners. This layered system protects against pornography, sexting, sextortion, and other online harms that spill into real-world danger. It's not punishment; it's protection. Freedom comes with responsibility, and safety is non-negotiable.

Our vigilance is backed by hard data. Adolescent mental health struggles are rising—and often tied to heavy phone and screen use. One in five teens has a diagnosed mental or behavioral condition. Surveys show four in ten feel persistently hopeless, two in ten have seriously considered suicide, and nearly one in ten has attempted it. Higher levels of screen time correlate with worse sleep, less exercise, and increased depression—especially when it replaces face-to-face connection. Those numbers justify strict boundaries.

Gaming is allowed in our home, but as a privilege—not an expectation. We ban graphic violence or sexual content for younger children and set strict time limits. For kids with conditions like Fetal Alcohol Spectrum Disorder, prolonged gaming can trigger negative behaviors. We've seen better results with active games like *Just Dance* that build movement and connection. Gaming in our home is curated, time-limited, and balanced with real-world skills and resilience.

And what fills the space left by fewer screens? Real life—messy, loud, and beautifully alive. Our kids climb trees, build forts, invent games, and yes, sometimes land us in the emergency room because they're outside learning, risking, and growing.

That may sound harsh until you consider the alternative: children are isolated behind screens, shaped by algorithms instead of real life. Our rules are born of love and urgency. Raising healthy, resilient kids in a wired world requires boundaries, accountability, and fierce commitment.

Call to Action

Right now, predators are online messaging children who look just like yours. Some pose as friends. Some offer gifts. Some patiently groom, waiting for the moment your guard slips. And here's the chilling truth: they don't have to break into your home. You hand them the key every time your child logs in.

Don't believe the lie: *"Not my kid."* Every parent who's said those words thought the same—until the day their child's photo was shared, their trust shattered, their innocence stolen.

Act tonight—not tomorrow. Take the phone. Take the tablet. Set rules. Lock privacy settings. Install Bark. Install Covenant Eyes. No excuses. No delays.

This is not optional. This is not an exaggeration. It is war for your child's safety, and predators are already fighting for them. The only question is: **will you fight harder?**

CHAPTER NOTES:

Chapter 6

Recognizing Warning Signs & Responding Early

Most parents believe they would know if their child is in danger. They imagine abuse would be obvious, predators easy to spot, and their child running to them the moment something felt wrong. The harsh truth? That's not how it happens. Predators count on parents being distracted, busy, and willing to explain away warning signs. Too often, they're right. By the time the truth surfaces, the damage is already done — and parents are left asking how they missed it.

Warning signs don't flash in neon lights. They arrive as whispers — quiet shifts that are easy to dismiss as "just a phase." A teen who suddenly drops out of activities they once loved. A once easygoing child who is now moody, secretive, or quick to anger. Grades slipping, meals skipped, nights spent awake. Headaches, stomachaches, or fatigue with no clear medical cause. Younger kids may suddenly cling, regress into behaviors like bedwetting, or fear certain people or places without explanation. Parents want to believe these are normal stages of growing up. Predators and abusers count on that denial. What looks like a phase may be evidence of grooming or abuse.

And grooming rarely looks like what parents expect. It doesn't start with violence — it starts with flattery. An older peer or adult gives a child special attention, gifts, or praise that makes them feel chosen. They introduce secrecy: *"Don't tell anyone, they wouldn't understand."* They slowly isolate the child from friends and safe adults. Online, the process moves faster: a friendly chat turns private, compliments become flirty, then come requests for photos, phone numbers, or a secret meeting. To a parent glancing across the room, it looks like a kid laughing at their phone. To the predator, it's the tightening of a trap.

The fallout of abuse can be devastating. Sudden fear. Unexplained injuries. Drastic changes in appearance or hygiene. Avoidance of certain people or places. Teens guarding their phones, inventing stories about new "friends," or showing up with money and gifts they can't explain. Parents chalk it up to adolescence — but secrecy and gifts don't protect children, they protect predators. Your gut may whisper that something is off. That whisper is almost always right.

And yet, even then, parents hesitate. They don't want to accuse wrongly. They hope it's nothing. But hesitation can cost a child their safety. Intervention is not optional — it's urgent. If a child is in immediate danger, call emergency services. For crises that aren't life-threatening, dial or text **988** for trained counselors. Suspected abuse or trafficking must be reported — and in many states, you're legally required to do so. Hotlines can connect families to shelter, legal support, and medical care.

When you confront a child you're worried about, the way you respond matters. Choose privacy. Speak calmly. Name what you've noticed: *"You seem withdrawn lately, and you've stopped seeing your friends."* Then listen more than you talk. Ask open questions. Don't shy away from the hard ones — asking directly about self-harm or abuse can save a life. Even small steps — removing dangerous means, creating a safety plan, connecting them with trusted adults — can interrupt a spiral. Programs like **Mental Health First Aid** prepare both parents and teens to step in before it's too late.

Behind closed doors lies one of the most hidden horrors: familial trafficking. Children may be coerced, traded, or sold by the very people meant to protect them. Out of fear, shame, or loyalty, they may never speak up — believing the nightmare is "normal" or deserved. Outsiders often mistake it for poverty or neglect. True safety only comes when professionals — child protection, law enforcement, healthcare, and social services — intervene to provide housing, counseling, and stability.

Here's the bottom line: **silence is the soil where abuse grows.** Intervention — even when it feels awkward, inconvenient, or uncertain — is the hinge between destruction and healing. Every time you notice, ask, and act, you slam the door on a predator. Every time you stay silent, you hold it open.

So, ask yourself: when your child's safety is on the line, do you want to be the parent who missed the signs — or the one who noticed, acted, and changed the outcome? Your choice today could be the difference between your child's silence and their survival.

Call to Action

Your child does not need you to be perfect — they need you to be present. They need you to pay attention when something changes, even when it feels easier to hope it's "just a phase." They need you to trust your instincts, even when the truth is frightening. The danger is real, and the cost of inaction is too high to ignore. Do not wait for proof. Do not wait for a confession. Do not wait for a crisis. When something feels wrong, that is your signal to move. Have the uncomfortable conversations. Check the phone. Ask the hard questions. Make the report. Reach out for help. Your child's safety is worth every awkward moment, every boundary you enforce, every question you ask. You are not overreacting.

27

You are protecting your child. Act now — because silence is where predators hide, and a parent who refuses to look away is their greatest threat.

CHAPTER NOTES:

Chapter 7

The Predators Playbook, Hiding in Plain Sight

Grooming – Online and in person:

Trigger Warning: This chapter contains descriptions of grooming, sexual assault, and exploitation. Some details may be difficult to read, but they are necessary to understand how predators operate and how to protect children.

It doesn't always look like danger. Sometimes it looks like trust.

A babysitter offers to stay late so you can run errands. They laugh with your child, bring small treats, and become the "fun one" in the house. Over time, hugs last a little longer. Tickling games become a little more physical. And then come the whispered words: *"This is just between us."* You don't notice the shift because from the outside, it still looks like kindness.

Meanwhile, in another home, a phone buzzes. Ping. A message from a new "friend" in an online game: *"Wow, you're really good at this. Wanna play again later?"* Your child lights up. Someone finally notices them, understands them. Soon, the chats move to private messages. The compliments grow sweeter. The friend becomes irreplaceable. And when they say, *"Don't tell your parents, they wouldn't get it,"* your child obeys.

This is grooming. It doesn't storm in with violence. It slides in quietly—through attention, affection, trust, or even love. It can happen behind a glowing screen, or it can be sitting at your dinner table. And it is always deliberate.

Predators are patient hunters. They study children, searching for cracks—loneliness, insecurity, family stress—and slip into those spaces. They pour on praise, gifts, and privileges until a child feels indebted. Then they test the edges: a "harmless" late-night text, a joke with sexual undertones, a hug that lingers too long. If no one notices, they push further. And with every step, they enforce secrecy: *"This is our little thing." "If you tell, you'll get in trouble." "I'll leave if you don't do this."*

By the time the lines are crossed, your child may not even see it as abuse—because the groomer has already twisted love into control, attention into obligation, affection into shame. That shame is the predator's strongest weapon.

And too often, parents don't see it. We dismiss secrecy as "normal teen behavior." We wave away mood swings, slipping grades, or withdrawal as "just a phase." We overlook unexplained gifts, a new older "friend," or a child suddenly avoiding someone we thought was safe. By the time we connect the dots, harm is already done.

Whether the predator enters through Wi-Fi, through a church door, through a school gym, or from within the family itself, the strategy is the same: gain trust, blur boundaries, enforce secrecy, tighten control.

The following case files show how grooming actually plays out—in living rooms, bedrooms, locker rooms, youth groups, and even within families. These are not rare stories. They are common patterns and they are happening all around us.

Case File 1: Grooming Inside the Home

The Johnsons trusted Megan, their longtime babysitter. She painted nails, whispered secrets, played "Truth or Dare," and told Sarah, *"You're my favorite. You're more mature than other kids your age."* The games grew riskier. Dares to change into pajamas while Megan "promised not to peek." Innocent-seeming selfies on her phone. Jokes with a sharp, suggestive edge. Hugs that lingered too long. Tickling that "accidentally" slid across private areas. When Sarah stiffened, Megan brushed it off: *"Don't be such a baby. This is just for fun."* Soon, secrecy was the price of keeping Megan's approval. *"If your parents knew, they'd freak out. They wouldn't understand us. Then I couldn't come over anymore. And you don't want to lose me, do you?"* Sarah felt trapped—flattered and scared—unsure if she had done something wrong. To her parents, Megan was still perfect. They never saw the manipulation tightening around their daughter like a net.

Why this matters: Grooming inside the home often hides behind affection and "fun." But when kindness turns into secrecy, dares, or boundary-blurring touch, it's not play—it's predation. By the time a child knows something is wrong, they're already silenced by fear and guilt.

Parent action steps:

Watch for secrets between your child and older youth/adults.

Don't dismiss "accidental" touches or off-color jokes—those are tests.

Teach: "No one should ever ask you to keep secrets from me."

Make it safe for your child to tell you *everything*, even if they think they'll get in trouble.

Reflection: Would you notice if your babysitter—or even a trusted family friend—was crossing these lines right in your living room?

Case File 2: Grooming Online

Lily, thirteen, was scrolling her tablet when a notification popped up. *"Hey, nice game last night. You're really good at this."* The boy's profile picture showed someone her age in a hoodie. Soon the messages were constant: *"You're funny." "You're more mature than other girls." "You're my best friend."* He asked about fights with her parents and the friends who left her out. Lily felt chosen. She guarded her device like treasure, deleting notifications before her mom could see. Then came the request: *"You should sneak out. We could grab fries. I'll keep you safe. Don't you trust me?"* When she hesitated, the messages piled up: *"You owe me." "Don't leave me hanging."* She thought she was talking to a boy her age. In reality, "Jay" was a grown man hundreds of miles away, grooming her to step outside her front door and into danger.

Why this matters: Many parents assume kids are safe at home. But predators don't need to knock—they slide in through a screen. Excessive messaging, secrecy, and pressure disguised as affection are red flags. By the time a child sneaks out, the trap is already set.

Parent action steps:

- Treat secrecy around devices as a red flag, not a phase.
- Watch for mood swings linked to online activity.
- Teach: "Anyone who cares about you will never ask you to hide things from me."

- Keep devices in open areas; review apps, contacts, and chat histories regularly.

Reflection: Would you catch it if someone online was texting your child late at night right now?

Case File 3: Grooming Within the Church

April, twelve, glowed when Pastor praised her voice: *"God gave you such a gift."* He noticed her shyness, made her feel chosen. Soon he offered private lessons. At first, it was music. Then gifts—like a journal with her name—paired with whispered instructions: *"This is our special time with God. Not everyone would understand."* He stood too close, rested his hand too long on her back, told her she was "set apart." He laced compliments with spiritual authority: *"God brought us together for a reason."* To April, it felt like trust. To outsiders it seemed like mentorship. But in reality, he was isolating her, weaving secrecy and dependence around her with holy-sounding words.

Why this matters: Predators exploit sacred spaces and authority roles because parents hesitate to question them. The flattery, the secrecy, the "special relationship" cloaked in religious language—all are calculated steps to groom a child while disarming suspicion.

Parent action steps:

- Teach your child: *No one gets private secrets with you, not even Pastors, teachers, or leaders.*
- Insist on transparency—no closed-door meetings with authority figures.
- Pay attention to flattery that singles your child out as "different" or "chosen."

33

- Trust your instincts—position or title does not equal safety.

Reflection: Would you question a pastor or leader if they wanted private "mentoring" time with your child? (I write much more on this next).

Case File 4: Grooming by a Coach

Ethan's parents were proud he was "Coach's favorite." Extra drills, extra encouragement, late-night texts. At first, it was about soccer. Then, *"You're more mature than the others." "I trust you."* Snacks after practice, car rides home, "our little tradition." Then the secrecy: *"Don't tell the others about our training—they wouldn't get it."* Adjustments during practice became touches that lingered too long. Hands on his waist, squeezes on his shoulder, brushing "accidents." When Ethan flinched, Coach laughed: *"Relax. Don't be so jumpy."* To parents, it looked like opportunity. To Ethan, it felt confusing and suffocating. To the coach, it was all part of a plan.

Why this matters: Authority figures like coaches use trust and opportunity as cover. Special treatment and secrecy are not mentorship—they're grooming. Escalation is gradual, making it harder for parents to notice until it's too late.

Parent action steps:

- Watch for favoritism that isolates your child from peers.
- Question secrecy around extra practices or "special coaching."
- Teach: "No adult should text you late at night or ask you to keep secrets."

- Attend practices when possible; verify extra sessions.

Reflection: Would you spot the difference between a dedicated coach and a grooming predator?

Case File 5: Grooming by a Sibling

Emma, twelve, adored her older brother Ryan, sixteen. He let her hang out in his room, borrow his phone, and watch shows she wasn't allowed. *"Don't tell Mom and Dad,"* he grinned. She felt grown-up, important. Soon, he shared personal struggles: *"You get me more than anyone."* His hugs lingered. Tickling turned uncomfortable. Hands stayed too long on her shoulders or waist. When she frowned, he teased: *"You're so sensitive."* Under a blanket watching movies, he pulled her closer. When she shifted away, he hushed her: *"Relax. Don't make this weird."* She froze—ashamed, confused, loyal. To her parents, it looked like sibling bonding. They never saw the slow erosion of boundaries into abuse.

Why this matters: Many children are groomed by siblings. Parents often miss it because it looks like normal family closeness. But secrecy, guilt, and escalating physical closeness are not sibling play. They're warning signs of harm.

Parent action steps:

- Don't dismiss discomfort between siblings as "just teasing."
- Monitor closed-door time and secrecy between children.
- Teach every child: *"Your body belongs to you—even family must respect your boundaries."*

- Believe and act if one child avoids or fears another.

Reflection: Could this already be happening in your home, hidden under the label of "siblings being siblings?"

Your Response Matters

If you suspect grooming, your response matters more than you know. Stay calm. Believe your child. Speak words that pierce the shame: *"I believe you. This is not your fault. You are safe with me."* Preserve evidence—messages, usernames, screenshots. Call law enforcement and child protective services. Seek medical care if needed and trauma-informed counseling. Never confront a predator alone.

Prevention will always be your greatest weapon. Start early. Make body-safety conversations as routine as brushing teeth. Teach your child the words for their body parts and the rules for their boundaries. Create tech rules and enforce them. Supervise one-on-one time—even with people you trust. Tell your child again and again: no one who loves them will ever ask them to keep unsafe secrets.

Because predators are not always strangers. Sometimes they are already in your child's circle of trust. Sometimes they are already in your home.

The question is not *if* someone will try. The question is *when*—and whether your child will know what to do, and whether you will see it in time.

Parent Reflection & Self-Audit: Could This Happen in My Home?

Predators count on one thing: parents believing *"not my child, not my house, not my circle."* The truth is that grooming thrives wherever adults let their guard down.

Before you close this chapter, stop and ask yourself these hard questions:

Trust & Boundaries

- Do I allow my child to spend time alone with older youth, babysitters, or adults without supervision?
- Would I notice if a "trusted" person started giving my child unusual gifts, attention, or secrecy?
- Have I made it clear that no adult — not even family — should ever ask my child to keep secrets?

Technology & Secrecy

- Do I know every app and contact on my child's phone or tablet?
- Would I notice if my child started guarding their device, deleting messages, or changing passwords?
- Have I told them clearly: "If someone online asks you to hide things from me, that's a danger sign?"

Behavior & Warning Signs

- Have I seen sudden changes in mood, grades, sleep, eating, or friend groups — and brushed them off as "a phase?"
- Do I pay attention when my child avoids certain people or places, even if I think that person is trustworthy?
- Do I act when my gut tells me something feels off, or do I hesitate out of fear of being wrong?

Conversations & Safety Nets

- Have I taught my child the words for their body and the right to say no — even to people they love?
- Do they know they can tell me *anything* without fear of punishment or blame?
- Do they have more than one safe adult they can go to if something feels wrong?

Call to Action

Circle the questions where your answer was *no* or *I'm not sure.* Those are the cracks predator's exploit. Close them — today. Set the rule. Check the device. Ask the hard question. Have the uncomfortable talk.

Every boundary you draw, every conversation you start, every instinct you act on is one less opening for a predator. Silence and delay are what they count on. Your vigilance is what stops them.

CHAPTER NOTES:

Chapter 8

Betrayal in the Pulpit

The sanctuary sings with familiarity: hymns rising, heads bowed, the steady cadence of a pastor's voice that has comforted generations. It is in that ordinary holiness that danger can hide. Most people who know Pastor Josh would describe him as a man you can call in an emergency day or night. The kind of man you would never suspect of harming a child. He smiles easily, remembers every family's name, prays with the grieving, and sits with struggling teens until they feel heard. He is the trusted face of the congregation — the last person most parents would imagine could be a predator. That trust is the weapon a groomer needs.

Annie is quiet in the way that makes adults look twice: attentive, gentle, eager to serve. When Pastor Josh singles her out, it feels like a blessing. He tells her she has a gift for listening, invites her to stay after youth group to help plan worship, offers to read scripture with her at the front of the church. Her parents glow with pride. The attention looks like affirmation. For many families, the story of a pastor noticing a child's gifts would end there — and that is exactly where the danger begins.

The grooming is not dramatic. It builds slowly, brick by brick, a ledger of small imbalances that add up to control. Pastor Josh begins to text her at odd hours: scripture at midnight, questions about private struggles at home. He schedules one-on-one Bible studies in his office, bringing coffee and warmth that make the room feel safer than it should. He praises her in a way that separates her from the other girls: "You understand things others don't," he tells her, casting their bond as unique and sacred. He reframes secrecy as holy — "This is between us" — and every secret is a stone pulled from the foundation of her safety. With each passing week, Annie shares less with her friends, less with her parents, and leans more heavily on the pastor.

Physical boundaries erode under the cover of pastoral care. A hug after a confession that lingers too long. A hand placed "for prayer" that rests in a place that feels wrong but is hard to name. A ride home that takes a longer route "so there's more time to talk." Each act can be excused away. Each is plausible, explainable, forgivable. And yet, each one chisels away at Annie's sense of normal. When she voices hesitation, fumbling toward words for her discomfort, Pastor Josh reframes her doubt as spiritual growth. He tells her that maturity requires difficult lessons, that trust means pushing past uncertainty, that questioning him is questioning God's will. Language meant to protect becomes the tool of manipulation.

The community's indifference shields the predator. When a youth leader or parent raises concern, they are met with calm reassurance: Pastor Josh is under stress, he has always been close with the teens, he's served faithfully for years. Suspicion is swallowed by the reflex to preserve reputation: handle it quietly, offer counseling, keep it inside the church. Forgiveness becomes a shield for the guilty. Silence is not neutrality; it is complicity.

The cost is devastating. Annie's faith becomes entangled with betrayal. The man who spoke to her about God becomes the man who taught her to distrust her own body and her own voice. She withdraws from her friends, her schoolwork unravels, and her nights fill with shame and fear. The very community that promised safety becomes a trap.

For many victims, this spiral deepens into depression, self-harm, and suicidal thoughts. And even when a case comes to light, the community's slow response and the pressure to forgive retraumatize survivors — while predators slip away to new pulpits, new towns, new victims. This is not about one "bad apple." It is about systems that fail to keep children safe. Churches that lack child-protection policies, that ignore background checks, that allow private meetings without oversight, that confuse spiritual authority with absolute trust — these are churches where predators thrive. When leaders hold unchecked power and communities prize reputation over truth, children lose both their safety and their voice.

Call to Action

Parents, take this as a summons to wakefulness. Trust is not abdication. Ask your church for written child-protection policies and demand they are enforced. Insist that mentoring and counseling happen in visible, supervised spaces, and that two adults are always present. Know who is working with your child; verify background checks and ask about training in safe boundaries. Teach your children plain, unapologetic words for inappropriate behavior. Not "It felt weird," but clear language they can use to name what happened. Make your home the place where a child's disclosure is met with belief and support, not doubt or anger. And if a child tells you something, act immediately: protect them, document, and report to civil authorities. Never leave it JUST to church leadership to "handle internally."

Communities must demand accountability. Require mandatory reporting. Push for external oversight that cannot be swept aside to protect reputation. Protect whistleblowers. Fund training for every staff member and volunteer. Build transparency into the DNA of the congregation.

A church that protects its image at the expense of its children is not serving God — it is endangering the very people it claims to shepherd.

This chapter is not meant to condemn faith or community; it is meant to shatter complacency. It is a warning: the most trusted face in the room can also be the most dangerous when power is weaponized.

Do not let a polished smile or a gentle sermon lull you into silence. Believe children. Demand safeguards. Refuse to let institutional comfort outweigh a child's safety. I will not remain silent, so you can remain comfortable — and neither should you.

Our Story: Causing to stumble

We are a family deeply rooted in Christian faith. We love our church and cherish our church family. That's why this is so hard to tell—because it happened to us. Not in our own church, but at a church-affiliated campground where we spent our summers.

My daughter worked there alongside the man who would harm her—a 27-year-old married man, the son of prominent youth leaders and church planters. To everyone else, including us he was respected, trusted, safe. That familiarity gave him access.

The grooming began as friendship: constant messages, lighthearted pictures, attention that seemed flattering. Slowly it shifted to secrecy and control. Then came the test. One afternoon in the gym, while she was playing basketball, he got her alone and forcefully kissed her—gauging her silence. She did not tell us right away. She brushed it off as an "oops," exactly what predators count on, hoping a child will minimize the violation instead of naming it.

But the next day, while she was cleaning the church, he assaulted her again. That time she knew—this was not an accident, not a mistake. It was wrong. And because she had been taught that she could always come to us, she told us immediately. Her courage in speaking up is what stopped him from continuing.

Afterward, he fled the campground for a few days. The district that oversaw the campground had safeguards in place. They were transparent, trauma-informed, and immediately launched an investigation. Their systems worked. The failure wasn't in the district—it was in the individual who chose to harm, and in his parents, who had hidden his prior transgressions in their own church.

The shock was not just that it happened, but that it happened where policies were strong, where precautions were taken. It was trust—his reputation, his family name—that became the weapon.

Why This Matters

Predators don't always hide in the shadows; often, they stand in the pulpit, coach the team, or work at the camp. They are "known," "respected," and trusted precisely because that trust disarms suspicion. Grooming rarely begins with violence. It begins with friendship, attention, and secrecy. Predators test boundaries, escalating only when they believe the child won't speak out.

Our daughter's story proves this: predators will often "test" a child first, gauging whether silence can be counted on. The difference between ongoing abuse and a predator being stopped often hinges on whether a child feels safe enough to tell the truth. That single disclosure can slam the door on further harm.

Even strong systems cannot eliminate risk. Policies, background checks, and rules are essential, but they are not bulletproof. Safety comes from vigilance—listening, noticing changes in your child, and refusing to believe that reputation equals protection.

Parent Action Steps

- Teach your child how grooming works. Explain that extra attention, secrecy, or gifts—even from trusted adults—can be red flags.
- Prepare them with language. Give them direct words to describe unwanted touch, secrecy, or control. Avoid euphemisms.
- Encourage immediate disclosure. Remind them: "If anyone—friend, leader, or pastor—does something that makes you uncomfortable, you can tell me right away. I will believe you."
- Stay alert in faith spaces. Camps, youth events, and church programs create relaxed environments where predators exploit familiarity. Supervision must always be questioned.
- Demand transparency. Ask how your church or camp handles allegations, and whether they report to civil authorities instead of only "handling it internally."

The truth is painful: predators count on your trust. They count on your belief that "this could never happen here." But it can. And when parents stay awake, aware, and equipped, predators lose the cover they need to strike.

Matthew 18:6 (NIV) states: *"If anyone causes one of these little ones—those who believe in me—to stumble, it would be better for them to have a large millstone hung around their neck and to be drowned in the depths of the sea."*

If this can happen to my family, it can happen to yours.

CHAPTER NOTES:

Chapter 9

Navigating Social Activities

The search for connection for our children should never mean a search for risk. When we allow them into youth groups, sports, or social circles, safety must guide every choice.

Start with the organization itself. Where do they meet? Are the facilities secure, well-lit, and accessible? What is the staff-to-child ratio? Are adults visible and accountable, or tucked away with unsupervised authority? Request written policies on background checks, child protection, and emergency procedures. Trustworthy organizations welcome questions and provide documentation openly. Hesitation, vague answers, or defensiveness are red flags. Whenever possible, drop in unannounced, observe interactions, and talk with other parents—patterns reveal more than polished words.

Choosing leaders and volunteers is less about charisma and more about character. Reliable programs require formal vetting: criminal background checks, reference calls, and training in youth safety. Look for adults who show calm authority, clear boundaries, and consistent follow-through—not just charm. Pay attention to how they handle conflict, set expectations, and maintain professional distance. Strong programs have explicit rules around physical contact, one-on-one time, and direct communication with minors. If teen leaders are involved, they must be supervised by vetted adults and only given responsibilities appropriate to their maturity and training.

Preparing your child for group dynamics is just as important as vetting adults. Equip them with clear language for consent and refusal. Practice simple phrases they can use under pressure until the words come naturally. Teach them to recognize different types of peer pressure—from teasing to exclusion to coercion. Encourage them to use the buddy system, check in with you regularly, and come to you if something feels off. Just as important, show them that disclosure will be met with calm support. Kids who expect anger, disbelief, or punishment will stay silent.

Inclusion and safety can—and must—coexist. Inclusion is not the absence of rules; it is the presence of consistent, protective standards. Advocate for accommodations your child might need—different communication styles, sensory adjustments, or mobility support—while insisting those accommodations never weaken safety protocols. True inclusion requires leaders who are proactive: intentional icebreakers, structured group roles, and closely supervised activities that prevent isolation and vulnerability.

When it comes to church youth groups, camps, or any social program, we must be bold enough to ask the hard questions. Bad things do happen in faith spaces too. Ask directly about background checks:

- What kind are run—criminal, fingerprinting, sex-offender registry—and how often?
- Who reviews the results, and how are concerns documented?
- Are teen volunteers screened differently than adults?
- What training in child safety or trauma awareness is required?

If the answers feel vague or defensive, take that as your answer. If it doesn't feel right to you as the parent, it is not right for your child.

Knowing when and how to step in matters. If there is immediate danger, remove your child, seek medical help if needed, and contact emergency services without hesitation. For serious but non-urgent concerns, document the details—who, what, when, where, and any witnesses. Bring concerns first to the program leader or safeguarding officer and request a formal follow-up. If the response is dismissive or inadequate, escalate to the governing body, licensing authority, or child protective services. Keep communication calm and factual, protect your child's privacy, and maintain records of all correspondence.

The truth is this: parents often sense something before they can fully name it. Trust that instinct. Your persistence, your questions, and your presence can be the barrier that stops harm before it starts. Connection is vital for our kids—but connection without vigilance is a gamble they should never have to pay for.

Parent Checklist: Questions Before You Leave Your Child

- Where does this group meet, and are the facilities safe and supervised?
- What is the staff-to-child ratio, and are adults visible at all times?
- Do you conduct background checks (criminal, fingerprint, sex-offender registry) on every staff member and volunteer? How often are they updated?
- How are teen helpers supervised, and what roles are they allowed to have?
- What child-protection and emergency policies are in place? May I see them in writing?
- How do you handle one-on-one interactions, texting, or private communication with minors?

- What training do leaders receive in child safety, trauma response, or behavior management?
- If a concern arises, what is the exact process for reporting and follow-up?
- Have you set up a code word for your child to use if there is an issue and they can't speak freely to let you know they need a way out?

If you feel stonewalled, rushed, or dismissed, trust your gut. A safe program never hides its safeguards.

CHAPTER NOTES:

Chapter 10

Human Trafficking – Familial and Online Risks

I am the mother of seventeen children. Eleven were adopted out of foster care. Five of those are survivors of human trafficking. Let that sink in. Five. And here's the truth that makes people gasp every time: none of them were harmed by strangers. Every single one was hurt by someone they knew, loved, and trusted.

When I share this, people look at me in disbelief. They want to believe trafficking is rare—that it happens overseas, in big cities, or in shadowy alleys. That it is the work of strangers. But the truth is much closer to home. For our five children, the traffickers weren't kidnappers. They weren't nameless predators. The traffickers were their own parents. My children weren't stolen off the street. They were sold at the dinner table, in the very homes where they should have been safe.

I wish I could tell you foster care caught it quickly. But it didn't, not for lack of trying but because human trafficking is like a thousand-piece puzzle you must put together. The only problem is that all the puzzle pieces are clear like glass, making it difficult to put together. Familial trafficking is often invisible. Case files get filled with words like "neglect," "behavioral problems" or "sexual abuse" while the truth—the selling, the exploitation—remains hidden. Children rarely have the words to explain it. They are too scared, too conditioned, or too ashamed to speak. For many, being sold feels like "normal life." By the time the truth surfaces, the damage is already deep. This doesn't mean child protection workers didn't care—it means the abuse was buried so well it sometimes took years before the pieces came together.

I see the scars every day. Some of my children flinched when I reached out to hug them. Others hid food under pillows because hunger had been used as punishment. One of my daughters couldn't sleep unless the closet light was on—not because of imaginary monsters, but because in her world the monsters walked right through the door. Even years later, I've held them through panic attacks so intense they couldn't breathe. I've listened as they whispered questions that should break every parent's heart: *"Why did my mom give me away?"* *"Why did my dad make me do that with people?"*

Adoption gave them safety, but safety is not the same as healing. Trauma rewires everything—how a child trusts, how they love, how they see themselves. Healing is slow. It takes years of steady love, therapy, and safe spaces before a child dares to believe they are worth protecting. But I've watched my children rebuild, piece by fragile piece. Their resilience is breathtaking.

This is what every parent and community must understand: trafficking is not rare, and it is not "somewhere else." It is here. In our schools, our churches, our neighborhoods, our homes. And it is online—sitting inside the phones we hand our children. Predators no longer need to break in; they slip quietly through Wi-Fi, through gaming apps, direct messages (DMs), and video chats. And sometimes the predator isn't even a stranger. Sometimes it's a family member, a coach, a pastor, or a trusted friend.

The signs are there—if we're willing to see them. A child pulling away. Sudden mood swings. Unexplained money or gifts. Dropping grades. Extreme secrecy online. Exhaustion. Too often, adults shrug these off as "just being a teenager." But for some kids, these signs are the only scream they know how to give.

Here's the reality no parent wants to face: it's not a question of *if* someone will try to prey on your child—it's *when*. The only questions are: will you notice, will your child trust you enough to tell you, and will you believe them when they do?

Five of my children were trafficked before they ever reached my home. They lost pieces of their childhood they will never get back. But today, they are safe. They are loved. And every single day I remind them: *You are worth protecting. You are worth fighting for. You are worth keeping safe.* Every child deserves that chance.

Trust your gut, speak up, and do not look away—because silence is what traffickers count on.

Parent Action Steps

- **Stop thinking "not my kid."** Trafficking does not discriminate. Your child is not immune because of where you live, your faith, or your family values.
- **Check their phones.** Don't just glance—look. Read texts. Scroll DMs. Check hidden folders. Predators thrive in secrecy.
- **Ask the awkward questions.** "Has anyone asked you for pictures?" "Has anyone touched you in a way that felt wrong?" "Do you feel pressured to keep secrets from me?" Your discomfort is nothing compared to your child's safety.
- **Don't assume they'll tell you.** Kids often hide abuse out of fear, shame, or manipulation. Your job is to notice the red flags they can't explain.
- **Look for changes.** Isolation. Mood swings. Sudden gifts. New "friends" you've never met. Lost interest

in things they used to love. Don't excuse it—investigate it.

- **Know who's in their world.** Friends, coaches, youth leaders, babysitters. Predators often come wrapped in trust and respect.

- **Control online access.** Phones, tablets, gaming systems—if it has Wi-Fi, it's a door into your child's life. Keep it open where you can see. Use parental controls.

- **Teach them to say "No."** Give your child words and confidence to reject secrecy, inappropriate touch, or pressure. Role-play it. Practice it.

- **Be their safe place.** If your child comes to you—even hesitantly—drop your anger and shock. Believe them first. Protect them fast.

- **Act immediately.** If you suspect trafficking, don't wait. Don't confront the predator yourself. Don't "handle it quietly." Call law enforcement. Call the National Human Trafficking Hotline:

If you suspect trafficking, don't wait. In the U.S., call the National Human Trafficking Hotline at **1-888-373-7888** or text **233733 (BEFREE)**. If a child is in immediate danger, call 911. Trust your gut, speak up, and do not look away—because silence is what traffickers count on.

CHAPTER NOTES:

Chapter 11

Matison's Story

How mental health promotes vulnerability

Matison didn't grow up neglected. She wasn't forgotten or unloved. She had it all: a good home, family vacations, and every sport you could imagine. She went to every dance, wore every uniform, and was celebrated at every milestone. She was cherished, supported, and poured into. By every measure, she had a life filled with love and promise.

Her mother, Amy, ran a hair salon, and some of Matison's sweetest memories were made there. Before big school dances, Matison and her friends crowded into Amy's shop, laughing, picking out styles, and letting Amy curl and pin their hair. Those moments—girls giggling, music playing, Amy's hands weaving love into every strand—captured the heart of their family life. Matison was not a forgotten child. She was adored.

But love at home couldn't shield her from what came next.

As she entered adulthood, Matison struggled with depression and anxiety. She married, became pregnant, and gave birth to a beautiful son. Then postpartum depression hit hard. This is a real darkness that many mothers face, but few speak about. It wrapped itself around her and began to consume her world.

She went to her doctor, desperate for help, only to be told medication would interfere with breastfeeding. She was advised to "give it time."

What she heard was this: *the help you need is not available.*

Then came COVID. The world shut down. Appointments were canceled, medications delayed, and mental health services collapsed. The one thing that might have steadied her was gone. The depression deepened, her marriage strained, her home unraveled—and she ended up across the country from her family, homeless and alone.

This is how vulnerability took root. Not from neglect, not from lack of love, but from the cracks created when illness is left untreated, and systems fail.

The lies of postpartum depression told her she was a burden, that her child would be better without her, that she was unlovable. And when the medical system confirmed those lies by brushing her aside, she was left with nowhere to turn.

That's when Matison sought relief on the streets. Drugs promised quiet, promised escape. But instead, they chained her. And in that weakened state, she met her trafficker.

He saw what others missed: a young woman who once had everything, now desperate for anything to numb her pain and voices in her head. He disguised exploitation as care, counterfeit love as safety. What began as "treatment" on the streets quickly became entrapment.

Matison didn't walk into the sex industry. She was pulled in—piece by piece—through the opening her mental health crisis created.

The girl who once twirled in dance dresses after Amy styled her hair—the girl who played every sport, took every vacation, and had a family cheering her on—never made it out.

Her vulnerability was weaponized against her. The cycle of drugs and exploitation became stronger than her ability to escape.

Matison's death was not the result of bad choices, nor the result of a family who failed her. They did everything that could have been done with the tools available to work with. Amy fought for her daughter, sought care, and loved her fiercely. But even then, the cracks in the system swallowed Matison.

Mental health struggles open doors that predators are quick to exploit.

- **Functional Impairment:** Depression and trauma cloud judgment, weaken defenses, and make it harder to cope with stress.
- **Isolation:** Stigma and shame push people away from their support systems, leaving them vulnerable and alone.
- **Exploitation:** Predators watch for those cracks—moments of despair, loneliness, or need—and step in with promises and counterfeit comfort.
- **Mental illness**: Doesn't just affect individuals. It ripples through families, weakening even the strongest bonds. A child who was once thriving can become vulnerable in a matter of weeks when mental health needs go unmet.

Carrying Matison's Legacy

Amy refused to let her daughter's story end in silence. Through Millstone Ministry, she carries Matison's memory into the very places where trafficking thrives.

She created Matison's Love Bags—simple bags filled with hygiene supplies, food, and survival items. But more than that, each one carries a lifeline: a card with a number

Amy answers day or night, and a message Matison needed to hear:

"You are not alone. You are worth saving. You are loved. You are enough."

These bags are hand-delivered into vulnerable areas of the community, places where traffickers hunt. They are a voice of hope in the shadows, keeping Matison's memory alive by reaching the very people she once stood among.

A Call to Action

If it could happen to Matison, it could happen to anyone.

- **Parents:** Don't wait for obvious signs. Ask hard questions. Watch closely. Refuse to let shame or silence cover your child's pain.
- **Communities:** Normalize and demand mental health care. Fight stigma. Fill the gaps before predators do.
- **Systems:** Stop dismissing mental health. Stop letting waitlists become death sentences. Healthcare must protect, not abandon.

Amy did everything she knew could be done, and still, her daughter was lost. That means the rest of us—neighbors, leaders, schools, churches, and lawmakers must do more.

Matison's life should have been saved. Her death is a warning. And her story demands action—before another family who "did everything right" loses everything anyway.

Matison Rokia Francis
1/13/1998 – 10/3/2022

CHAPTER NOTES:

Chapter 12

Setting Boundaries and Rules

Boundaries are not optional. They are the life-preserving guardrails that separate safety from chaos. In a culture that blurs lines, your child will only learn what safety looks like when you show it. Rules aren't about control — they're about protecting your child from predators, accidents, addictions, and consequences that can last a lifetime.

The hard truth is that when parents hesitate, minimize, or let things slide, risks expand. Predators and dangerous situations exploit gaps: unlocked doors, unsupervised online time, blurred family norms. Boundaries only work when adults model and enforce them consistently. Children model what they see: if you treat rules as negotiations or optional, they will too.

I've sat with families who thought love alone was enough. One mother brought a new boyfriend into her home soon after meeting him. She wanted companionship; her daughter paid the price. That man crossed lines, tested boundaries, and eventually abused her. The mother still wonders if one hard rule — clearer vetting, no overnight stays, or enforced device limits — could have prevented years of trauma. This is the cost of leaving gaps.

Age-appropriate boundaries:

Infants (0–12 months): Safety = total dependence.

Non-negotiables: sleep on a firm mattress, no loose bedding, no unattended time on raised surfaces, small objects and chemicals locked away, rear-facing car seats for every ride. Childproof before they crawl. Limit who has access to your baby—vet caregivers and visitors, never leave your infant alone with unfamiliar adults, and avoid unsupervised adult-only time with your child. Predators look for opportunity and the youngest are the most vulnerable. Remember infants have temperaments—some are easily overstimulated or need extra soothing—so establish consistent routines, respond promptly to distress, and ensure every caregiver follows the same calming and care strategies. Communicate rules to every caregiver—no exceptions.

Toddlers (1–3 years): Zero hazard awareness and relentless testing.

Non-negotiables: Use firm, simple commands ("Hold my hand," "Hot—don't touch"). Physical barriers (gates, locks, outlet covers) are mandatory. Start body-safety basics: name private parts, teach "no" to unsafe touch, and practice simple refusal scripts. Limit who has unsupervised access—vet caregivers and never leave toddlers alone with unfamiliar adults; predators exploit lapses in supervision. Account for toddler temperament (impulsivity, clinginess, sensory sensitivity) by keeping routines, giving clear limits, and requiring every caregiver to enforce the same rules.

Preschoolers (3–5 years): Can follow multi-step rules but lack impulse control.

Non-Negotiables: Can follow multi-step rules but still lack impulse control and are easily influenced. Practice emergency behaviors ("stop, look, listen"), teach simple stranger-safety scripts ("I don't go with people I don't know; I find a parent or trusted adult"), drill fire and water safety, and use role-play. Begin consent education—teach "ask before touching" and how to say "no" to unsafe touch. Limit and vet who has access—never leave preschoolers alone with unfamiliar adults and avoid unsupervised adult-only time; predators exploit casual opportunities. Account for temperament (shyness, clinginess, high curiosity) with predictable routines, short practice sessions, and consistent enforcement by every caregiver.

School-age (6–12 years): Responsibility increases; guardrails remain essential.

Non-Negotiables: Responsibility increases but guardrails remain essential. Devices should be charged in a central location—not bedrooms—and parents should know passwords and monitor accounts; teach digital citizenship (privacy, respect, permanence of posts) and that adults or friends should never ask them to keep unsafe secrets. Homework before screens; encourage daily outdoor play and face-to-face friendships. Vet playdates and anyone who spends time with your child—never leave them alone with unfamiliar adults and supervise parties or overnight events; predators exploit gaps in supervision. Watch for temperament signs (risk-taking, peer-pressure susceptibility, or anxiety) and tailor rules and conversations accordingly. Consequences must be immediate and logical; privileges expand only with consistent responsibility.

Teenagers (13+): Stakes rise—driving, dating, alcohol, sex, unsupervised online access.

Non-Negotiables: Stakes rise—driving, dating, alcohol, sex, and unsupervised online access. Set negotiated curfews and clear rules for dating and overnight stays but keep non-negotiable protections (no unsupervised visits with new partners; no phones in bedrooms or bathrooms). Parents should know apps, passwords, and accounts until teens prove responsibility; restrict unsupervised access to their devices for younger teens and perform periodic checks to spot grooming or risky behavior. Have explicit talks about consent, sexting, pornography, and legal consequences; teach how to report uncomfortable situations. Watch temperament (impulsivity, mood swings, risk-taking) and tailor boundaries accordingly. Broken rules mean immediate, proportional loss of privileges when safety is at risk—consistency protects them.

Parent Action Steps: Boundaries That Protect

- Model what you demand. Children copy how you set limits for yourself—consistency from adults is essential.
- No phones or gaming devices in bedrooms or bathrooms. Ever. These private spaces are where predators and addictive behaviors thrive.
- Vet every adult you bring into your child's life. Don't allow new partners or temporary caregivers unsupervised access without time, trust, and discernment.

- Communicate rules clearly and often. A rule unspoken is a rule unenforced. Make sure your child and every caregiver know what's allowed and what isn't.
- Match rules to development, not desires. Adjust guardrails as children grow but keep core protections unchanged.
- Enforce consequences immediately and proportionally. If broken rules have no cost, boundaries lose power.
- Stay consistent. Rules shouldn't change with your mood or stress. Boundaries that bend today are gone tomorrow.

Boundaries don't make you a strict parent. They make you a safe parent.

CHAPTER NOTES:

Chapter 13

Sleepovers

Sleepovers often *feel* safe, but nights away concentrate risk: supervision thins, peer pressure rises, and opportunities for boundary violations multiply. Clinicians often cite that a large proportion of child sexual abuse incidents involve other minors—commonly quoted around **70%**. The exact number varies by study, but the trend is clear: children are most often harmed not by strangers, but by people already inside their circle.

That's what makes sleepovers risky. When kids are away overnight, supervision loosens, older siblings and their friends drift in, new faces show up who parents may not even know, and boundaries blur. Add late nights, lowered inhibitions, and peer pressure, and the environment is primed for danger—whether it's sexual abuse, bullying, exposure to pornography, substance use, sneaking out, or reckless dares.

The Safety Checklist

Before you hand over a toothbrush, demand clear, named answers—no exceptions. I understand these are a lot of questions. If you know the family where your child is staying chances are you know the answers. If you do not, in my opinion your children should not be staying there.

- Who will be awake overnight? (names, ages, relationship to the host).

- Where will my child sleep—and with whom?
- Will older siblings, their friends, or outside guests be present? If so, who?
- What other adults may come and go, and are they vetted? (boyfriends, relatives, neighbors, etc.).
- What are the rules for phones, screens, and internet access?
- Are cameras or monitoring devices in the home?
- Are there firearms, alcohol, or unlocked storage areas—and how are they secured?
- How will my child reach me at any time?
- Who will handle medical needs, medications, or allergies?

If you cannot get *direct* answers, the answer is no. Vague, defensive, or evasive responses are not quirks of personality—they are **red flags and deal-breakers.**

Non-Negotiables

Certain risks mean the sleepover ends instantly. One strike is enough.

- Mixed sleeping with older teens or unsupervised adults.
- Unvetted people drifting in and out of the house.
- Restrictions on parent calls, cameras, or check-ins.
- Unfiltered adult content in the home.
- Any pressure for secrecy.
- Excessive, intrusive, or boundary-testing behavior.
- Early signs of grooming.

If the host argues or pushes back, **that alone is your answer: no.**

Peer Pressure Risks

Even without predators in the home, kids can still be pulled into unsafe behavior. Late-night dares, unsupervised internet use, sneaking out, watching pornography, experimenting with substances, or copying what older kids are doing—it all happens most often when adults are asleep or absent.

Children crave belonging, and peer pressure can silence their instincts. At sleepovers, the desire to fit in can override everything they know about safety. That's why prevention isn't just about the host family—it's about the environment, the crowd, and the pressures your child will face when you're not there.

Preparing Your Child

Rules on paper don't keep children safe—skills do.

Prepare them now.

- **Rehearse short, automatic responses**: "No." "My parent needs me." "I'm calling home."
- **Set a family code word**: a single phrase that means *pick me up now, no questions asked.* Practice until it's second nature.
- **Teach body safety**: correct names for private parts, no "fun secrets," and the right to leave any room at any time.

Send your child prepared with a small emergency kit: flashlight, charger, printed emergency contacts, medical notes, comfort item, and the host's full address and phone number. Agree on at least one parent check-in before the night begins.

If you prefer written confirmation, keep it simple:

"Thanks for hosting. Quick questions before tonight: Who will be awake overnight (names/ages)? Where will [child's name] sleep and with whom? Will any overnight guests, older siblings, or teens 16+ be present? What are your rules for phones/screens and parent check-ins? Please send your address and best number."

If the host bristles at that message **cancel the sleepover.**

When the Code Word Comes

If your child uses the code word, your response is immediate.

- Confirm the word.
- Stay calm: ask if they are safe, where they are, and whether they can talk.
- Give direct instructions: "Leave the room." "Go to the kitchen." "Call 911."
- Tell them you are coming and give a clear ETA.

Do not call the host — go immediately. Calling could put your child at greater risk if the host scolds them for contacting you. If you must call, only say you are en route — do not negotiate or delay. Do not leave your child waiting while you "talk it through." Go yourself or send a trusted, identified adult.

If Something Goes Wrong

- If harm occurs, move fast.
- Remove your child immediately.
- Document names, times, messages, and details.

- Seek medical care quickly if injury or forensic evidence is possible.
- Use a child advocacy center for interviews—don't repeatedly question your child at home.
- Report criminal behavior or sexual contact to police and child protective services.

And above all **believe your child.**

Safer Alternatives

- Friendship doesn't have to mean sleepovers at all.
- Host the event at your home, where supervision is yours.
- Plan evening hangouts that end before bedtime.
- Limit sleepovers to families you know deeply and who commit to your safety checklist.

Next chapter: how our family's version of a sleepover rewrites every rule you've ever known.

CHAPTER NOTES:

Chapter 14

The Great Sleepover Debate

This chapter will raise questions, and I am okay with that. We are very clear in our home: **we do not do typical sleepovers.** Our children are allowed to stay overnight in exactly two homes They are families we've known for years, whose caregiving, routines, and values mirror ours—and that's it.

Here's the truth: in our family, sleepovers don't look like everyone else's. We do allow children to stay at our home, where we know the supervision and rules but that is very limited.

I know too much. I've seen the police reports, the sexual and physical abuse cases, the ER visits where "the kids were supposed to be sleeping." And if I'm honest, I remember what I got into at sleepovers with my childhood best friend Jamie. The difference? Back then, the world was different. We roamed neighborhoods without fear. Parents trusted doors unlocked.

That world is gone. Risks are sharper, predators are closer, and peer pressure is more dangerous than ever. Kids don't need an opportunity—they need protection.

Here are just a few case studies that I personally know about, some have been in the news.

Case Study: April

April went to spend the night at her friend Emily's house. Before the visit, April's mother confirmed that an adult would be present and supervising. Later that evening, Emily contacted two boys, Caiden and Micah, and the girls secretly left the home to meet them. While at the local park, Caiden sexually assaulted April. Shocked and frightened, April and Emily returned to the house and disclosed to Emily's mother what had happened. Instead of immediately seeking help, Emily's mother discouraged them from reporting the assault, fearing involvement from law enforcement or child protective services.

The girls were pressured into silence. In the months that followed, April's behavior began to change. She withdrew, struggled emotionally, and showed signs of distress. Only then did the truth surface, after her mother recognized that something was deeply wrong and gently began asking questions. With support, April was finally able to disclose the assault.

Case Study: Sleepover Incident

A group of middle school girls gathered for a sleepover at their friend Lily's home. Lily's father was present in the house and appeared friendly and attentive, offering snacks and soft drinks throughout the evening. The girls noticed that the drinks tasted slightly unusual but attributed it to the brand. Shortly after, several of them began to feel extremely drowsy, disoriented, and unable to stay awake.

One of the girls managed to text her older sibling, who recognized the signs of drug intoxication and alerted their parents. Emergency services were contacted immediately. Toxicology screens later showed that the father had added benzodiazepines to the girls' beverages, a drug commonly used to induce sedation and lower a person's defenses. The prompt call for help prevented further harm.

The investigation revealed that the father had been grooming the situation for access and control. He was arrested and charged, and the children were provided medical evaluation and trauma-informed counseling.

Case Study: Abigail

Abigail was having a slumber party with three close friends. Later that night, the group began playing *truth or dare*—a game that, at their age, often pushes boundaries. During the game, Abigail was dared to send an inappropriate photo to a boy from school. The girls pressured her, assuring her it was "just a joke" and "he won't show anyone." Feeling embarrassed and afraid of being judged, Abigail agreed and sent the photo.

The boy did not keep it private. He saved the image and shared it with others at school. Within days, Abigail began receiving messages demanding more photos. When she refused, the boy threatened to send the picture to more students, teachers, and even her family. Abigail felt trapped. She tried to handle it alone, believing she would get in trouble if she told an adult. Her behavior changed—she became anxious, withdrawn, and hesitant to go to school.

Only after her mother gently asked about the sudden shift in mood did Abigail break down and reveal what had happened. Once the adults became involved, the situation was reported, and Abigail and her family received support through trauma-informed counseling and school intervention. The boy's actions were addressed through legal and school disciplinary channels.

So, when it comes to sleepovers, our family refuses to follow the crowd. We choose safety, even if it looks radical to other parents. Because my child's safety is not up for debate, and it is not worth gambling on what "everyone else" is doing.

And this is where we separate from what the world calls normal—because the way we do sleepovers, and the way we handle overnight safety, is nothing like what you've seen before.

This boundary is not about being difficult; it is about being deliberate. It is about safety, rest, and stability in a world that constantly chips away at all three.

Why We Say No

Handing your child over for a night means handing over authority for **safety, supervision, and discipline** to another household. That's not a small decision. Trust must be earned, proven, and continually observed—not assumed because a family seems "nice." I am not looking to win a popularity contest; in fact, I just do not care. If people are mad at the choices we make to do our best to keep our children safe so, be it.

Sleepovers magnify risks:

- **Older siblings and their friends.** Parents often overlook that older teens may invite peers who don't belong around your child. Siblings may not share the moral compass you teach, leaving your child vulnerable. Sleepovers and slumber parties can be breeding grounds for risky or inappropriate behavior.
- **Unvetted adults.** Boyfriends, girlfriends, cousins, neighbors and casual visitors may drift in and out — you might not know who's in the home after dark. This creates vulnerability beyond the safe environment you've vetted for your child; you simply cannot control or vet people who may stop by.
- **Peer pressure.** Kids do dumb things when they want to fit in—sneaking out, vaping, sexting, dares, porn,

or even just "stupid pranks" that can scar or humiliate another child.

- **Sleep deprivation and routines.** A strange bed, too much sugar, late-night screens, or no rules at all leave children overstimulated, overtired, and emotionally raw for days.

When you add it all up, the "fun" of a sleepover comes at a cost that is far too high.

The Numbers Parents Don't Hear

- **Most abuse is not by strangers.** About 50% of abusers are trusted non-family members; about 40% are family members. Only 10% are strangers.
- **Age of highest risk:** 7–15 years old.
- **Prevalence:** Globally and in the U.S., some studies indicate that up to **25-30% of girls** and **5-15% of boys** face sexual abuse before adulthood.
- **Peer-to-peer abuse:** Estimates suggest around 70% of child sexual abuse is by other minors. That means most danger isn't from the "creepy adult"—it's from another kid in the room.
- **Sleepovers/slumber parties:** Many incidents of child sexual abuse occur in private residences, and because child-on-child abuse is peer-perpetrated, sleepovers can be a common setting for unreported abuse.

Add to that pornography, which floods peer culture:

- Average age of first exposure: **11 years old.**
- ~93% of boys and ~62% of girls report seeing porn by adolescence.

- Many teens treat porn as normal—and often pressure others to watch or imitate what they've seen.
- This is what our kids are walking into at 10 p.m. when parents "think the kids are sleeping."

Our Family's Rule

Our rule is simple: **no traditional sleepovers.**

Our children are not isolated—they are thriving in friendships. But they are thriving within safe, predictable boundaries.

When people push back, we respond kindly but firmly: "We don't do sleepovers, but we'd love to host a movie night or playdate."

By framing it as a family rule, not a judgment, we remove debate and show our kids that boundaries are normal, not negotiable.

Safety Beyond Our Home

Even when our kids are away during the day, we have a **code word**—a phrase they can drop into any conversation that signals *I need you to come get me right now.* Something ordinary like, "Hey Mom, what's for dinner?" lets them ask for rescue without tipping off anyone else. If that word comes through by text or call, we leave—no hesitation, no questions.

It's one of the simplest tools you can give your child: a private lifeline that says, *you are never stuck, and you are never alone.*

Are Sleepovers Worth It?

Some call them a rite of passage. I call them unnecessary risk. There is no evidence that sleepovers build stronger friendships than late-night hangouts, after-school activities, or family-hosted events. But there is overwhelming evidence that one "fun night" can open the door to situations children are not prepared to handle—situations that can leave scars for life.

You cannot remove every risk from your child's life. But you can refuse to hand them unnecessary ones. And that's exactly what a sleepover is: **a gamble with your child's safety that is never worth the odds.** One night of fun is not worth a lifetime of trauma.

Safer Alternatives

Want the fun without the danger? Try:

1. **Late Over / Late Night** — Friends come for games and snacks but go home before bedtime.
2. **Sleep Under** — Pajamas, movies, popcorn, then home to their own beds.
3. **Breakfast Bash** — A morning or brunch party where kids wear pajamas and eat pancakes.
4. **Themed Nights** — Craft parties, game nights, or movie marathons with a set end time.
5. **Drive in movie night** — We have a large blow-up outdoor movie screen; a backyard movie night is always a win with kids. Throw in what my kids call Unicorn Popcorn (popcorn with different candy in it) and a Slushie and it's a hit.

Kids laugh, bond, and make memories—without handing their safety over to the unknown.

Final Word

This isn't paranoia. It's protection.

Every family must make their own decision, but for us, this is the only one that makes sense. We are not raising our children to be afraid—we are raising them to be safe, resilient, and free to thrive without carrying scars from risks we could have prevented.

And that's why, in our home, the sleepover debate isn't really a debate at all. It's settled.

Traditional Sleepovers don't happen here. Period.

CHAPTER NOTES:

Chapter 15

Navigating Youth Groups and Social Activities

The search for connection should never mean a search for risk. When placing children in youth groups and social activities, safety must shape every choice. Evaluate organizations, select trustworthy leaders, prepare your child, and know how to act if something goes wrong.

I know this chapter is long and there's a lot of information to take in — that's intentional. Think of this process like interviewing someone for a corporate job: you wouldn't hire for an important role without asking detailed questions, checking references, and observing performance.

The biggest job of all is keeping our children safe, so treat screening and oversight with the same thoroughness and seriousness. You can't assume the work has been done for you — make sure of it yourself.

Evaluate the organization

- Know where meetings and events are held; prioritize secure, accessible facilities.
- Ask for written policies on background checks, child protection/safeguarding, emergency procedures, and incident reporting.
- Ask about staff-to-child ratios and supervision practices. Two adults per small group and no isolated one-on-one contact are good standards.
- Visit sessions (unannounced when possible), observe interactions, and speak with parents, volunteers, and

current participants — patterns matter more than a single conversation.

- Trust organizations that welcome questions and share policies; hesitancy, vagueness, or refusal to provide references is an early warning sign.

Selecting leaders and volunteers

- Prioritize programs requiring formal vetting: criminal background checks, sex-offender/abuse registry checks, reference verification, and documented training in child safety and behavior management.
- Ensure teen leaders are supervised by fully vetted adults and have responsibilities appropriate to their age and training.
- Look for adults who model calm authority, set clear boundaries, follow through on rules, and maintain professional distance. Pay attention to how leaders handle conflict and set expectations.
- Physical-contact policies, rules for one-on-one interactions, and clear communication channels with caregivers should be explicit and written.

Preparing your child

- Teach simple, rehearsed language for consent and refusal and practice scenarios until responses become reflexive.
- Teach children to recognize pressure (teasing, exclusion, coercion) and manipulative behaviors, to use a buddy system, and to check in frequently.
- Encourage open reporting: respond calmly and supportively to disclosures. Children are less likely to speak up if they fear anger, disbelief, or punishment.

- Build social skills that reduce risk: setting respectful boundaries, seeking adult help early, and identifying trustworthy adults.

Inclusion without compromising safety

- Inclusion requires consistent safety rules, not the absence of rules.
- Advocate for accommodations (communication differences, sensory needs, mobility) while insisting safety protocols apply to everyone.
- Proactive leaders use structured roles, intentional icebreakers, and supervised mixed-ability activities to reduce isolation and vulnerability.

Asking the hard questions

- Be direct and respectful when speaking with leaders. Explain you're ensuring your child's safety and ask for written policies and specifics (types of background checks, frequency of rechecks, who reviews results, and whether volunteers/teens are screened differently).
- Request to see the screening policy or a summary and follow up on any hesitancy or vagueness.
- If it doesn't feel right, trust your instincts. If something about the program, leader, or situation feels wrong to you as a parent, it's not right for your child. Your advocacy and insistence on transparency protect your child and others.

When and how to step in

- **Imminent danger:** act immediately. Remove your child, seek medical help if needed, and contact emergency services.
- **Serious but non-urgent concerns:** document who/what/when/where and any witnesses; speak first with the program leader or designated safeguarding officer and request a formal follow-up.
- **Inadequate response:** escalate to the organization's governing body, licensing authority, or child protective services. Keep communications factual, protect your child's privacy, avoid public accusations, and keep records of all interactions.

Sample questions to ask:

Screening & training

- Do you perform criminal, sex-offender, and child-abuse registry checks? How often are they repeated?
- Do you check references? Who reviews screening results?
- What child-protection, mandated-reporting, first-aid, and behavior-management training do staff receive and how often is it refreshed?

Supervision & policies

- What are your adult-to-child ratios by age? Are two screened adults present for each small group?
- Do you have a written child-protection/safeguarding policy? Can I see it?

- What are your policies on one-on-one meetings, rides, and physical contact?

Logistics & emergencies

- What are arrival/pickup procedures and how do you verify authorized adults? What happens if an unauthorized person arrives?
- What are the rules for off-site trips and overnight events? How are drivers and vehicles vetted? What permission forms are required?
- How do you handle allergies, medications, EpiPens, or inhalers? Are staff trained to respond to medical emergencies?

Reporting & communication

- Who is the designated child-protection person? How are suspected abuse reports handled with authorities and parents?
- How will you contact me during events or emergencies? Will I have the leader's contact information?

Behavior, privacy & volunteers

- What discipline methods are used? Are physical punishments allowed? How is bullying handled?
- What rules govern staff contact with youth on social media? Do you post photos/videos and how is consent obtained?
- How are occasional helpers or guest speakers screened? Are background-checked leaders always present?

- Do you keep records of incidents, injuries, and volunteer screening? Can parents access relevant incident reports involving their child?

For my child specifically

- How will you accommodate my child's medical, behavioral, or emotional needs?
- Which staff member will be directly responsible for them?

Quick red flags

- No written policies or refusal to share them.
- Vague answers about background checks, one-on-one supervision, or ratios.
- No clear pickup verification process.
- No plan for medical emergencies or lack of first aid/CPR training.
- Resistance to follow-up on concerns or a pattern of dismissing parent questions.

Your involvement—asking clear questions, observing programs, preparing your child, and documenting concerns—creates the conditions where young people can belong and thrive without compromising safety.

If staff or leaders respond to your safety questions with annoyance, defensiveness, or impatience, take that as a serious warning sign — imagine that same reaction when a safety lapse or a predator appeared, and consider that something important might have been missed. If the program leaders won't make the time to answer basic safety questions or become hostile when you ask, move on to a group that will prioritize transparency and your child's safety.

CHAPTER NOTES:

Chapter 16

Teaching Children About Touch and Consent

This chapter discusses sexual abuse and investigative procedures. If a child is in immediate danger, call emergency services now.

We often unknowingly train children to prioritize others' expectations over their own comfort. Commands like "give Uncle Billy a hug" or "kiss Grandma" treat children's bodies as props and teach obedience before self-awareness. Picking up a resistant child, forcing an embrace, or laughing off protests communicates that an adult's wishes trump a child's "no." When refusal is called "rude" or "selfish," children learn that upsetting an adult is worse than protecting their own body. Those lessons increase vulnerability to grooming later on. If we don't teach our children that it is okay to say "NO" to physical touch, the chances of them feeling like they can say "NO" to potential inappropriate touch one day is going to be a lot harder.

Teach the right words — and why it matters. Use correct anatomical names in calm, routine conversation. Age-appropriate, matter-of-fact terms remove ambiguity and empower children to report abuse precisely. Introduce penis, testicles, vulva, vagina, anus, buttocks, breasts (or chest) and say them without shame. "Private parts" is shorthand but not sufficient when a child needs to report something specific. Euphemisms like "cookie" or "popsicle" can be misunderstood or minimized and delay protective action.

Normalize anatomy while keeping explanations brief and non-sexual. Use terms during hygiene, diapering, or medical care. Praise children when they use the correct words and gently correct euphemisms: "We call that the penis. Thanks for telling me."

How correct language changes outcomes — forensic interviewing examples

These short, sanitized examples show how vague language and leading questions can derail an investigation, while neutral prompts and anatomical language preserve clarity. They are for parenting and training purposes only — do not attempt to conduct a forensic interview yourself.

Failed interview — euphemisms and leading questions

Context: A seven-year-old tells a parent, "Uncle Billy touched my cookie." The parent, alarmed but unsure, asks many questions before reporting. At school, a teacher asks leading yes/no questions.

Teacher: "Did he take off your clothes?"
Child (confused): "No?"
Teacher: "Did he touch you on your cookie?"
Child (unsure): "Maybe…"
Teacher: "Was it under your clothes?"
Child (frightened by the tone): "I don't know."

Problem: The euphemism ("cookie") is interpreted differently, and repeated, leading questions pressure the child and suggest answers. By the time professionals see the case, the child may retract or be too confused to give a clear account; physical evidence may be lost, and the case is weakened.

Effective forensic approach — neutral prompts and anatomical aids

Context: Same disclosure, but the child had been taught anatomy and a parent reported calmly. A trained forensic interviewer engages.

Interviewer: "Can you tell me everything that happened from the start to the end, in your own words?"
Child: "Uncle Billy was at our house. He asked me to sit with him. He put his hand down my pants."
Interviewer: "Can you show me where he put his hand?" [Offers an anatomically correct diagram or doll for the child to point to.]
Child (points to the vulva area): "Here."
Interviewer (clarifying without suggesting): "Thank you. Is there anything else that happened after that?"
Child: "He told me not to tell. He said it was our secret."

Why this works: The child used clear language or pointed to a diagram; the interviewer used broad, nonleading prompts. The disclosure remained the child's own words, preserving the account for protection, medical care, and possible prosecution.

Additional short variations (showing the same principle in different settings)

School staff context — why neutral phrasing matters

Failed version: A counselor asks, "Did he touch your cookie under your clothes?" The child, unsure what "cookie" means and feeling pressured, answers yes/no without detail.

Better version: A trained school interviewer asks, "Can you tell me what happened when you were with Uncle Billy?" If the child uses a word the adult doesn't know, the interviewer follows with neutral prompts such as, "Can you show me where that is on this picture?" This keeps the child's language intact and avoids suggesting answers.

Pediatrician context — turning a worried phrase into clarity without leading

Scenario: A parent brings a child who says, "Someone touched my private spot."

Ineffective response: Repeatedly pressing, "Who touched you? Where exactly?"

Effective response: The pediatrician says calmly to the child, "Thank you for telling me. Can you tell me where that was?" and offers an anatomical diagram or asks the child to point on their own body (without removing clothing). The clinician documents the child's words and points and immediately reports and refers for forensic evaluation and medical care.

Coach / after-school volunteer — boundary testing and disclosure

Scenario: A child confides to a coach about uncomfortable touches.

Ineffective response: The coach tries to solve it in private or encourages the child to "keep it calm" to avoid upsetting parents.

Effective response: The coach says, "I'm glad you told me. I believe you. I need to get you help and tell people whose job it is to keep kids safe." Then follows mandated reporting procedures and stays with the child until appropriate help arrives.

Online/text disclosure — why correct words help even remotely

Scenario: A teen messages a friend: "He touched my chest."
Ineffective response: The friend panics and asks vague, repeated questions.

Effective response by friend: "I'm sorry that happened. I believe you. Can you tell a trusted adult, or I can help you contact one?" Encourage the teen to use clear language when reporting and to save screenshots, then support them in reporting to a trusted adult or authorities. Encourage seeking a trained professional for the next steps.

Why parents should not perform forensic interviews

Your job is to believe, support, keep the child safe, and report to professionals. Repeatedly pressing for graphic details or asking leading questions can traumatize the child and contaminate memory; it can also jeopardize legal processes. Always tell the child you will get them help, then contact child protective services and law enforcement or a mandated reporter in your community.

Practical, age-appropriate phrases and actions

Preschoolers (3–5)

- **Teach:** "This is my body. My private parts are private."
- Use simple anatomical labels for bathing-suit areas.
- **Phrases:** "No. I don't like that. Stop." "I will tell my mom/dad."
- **Action:** Step back, put hands up, leave the room, find a trusted adult.
- **Practice & Rehearse:** "If someone tries to touch where your bathing suit covers, what do you say?" Then practice stepping away and finding a trusted adult.

Early elementary (6–9)

- **Teach:** clear anatomy and the difference between safe and unsafe touches.
- **Phrases:** "Stop. Don't touch my vagina/penis/butt." "That made me feel scared. I'm going to tell my parent."
- **Role-play:** Practice calm use of the words and leaving to tell a trusted adult.
- **Practice:** "Please stop. Don't touch my chest. I'm going to tell."

Older children and teens (10+)

- **Teach:** consent in relationships, boundaries, and online safety.
- **Phrases:** "I didn't agree to that. Stop. If you do it again, I will report it."

- Encourage a family safety code word or a preset contact for quick removal from a situation.
- **Practice:** Rehearse a short script for peer pressure: "I'm not comfortable. We're done. I need to go." Practice texting a preset contact or using the safety word.

Stand Up and ROAR

Many Child Advocacy Centers and child-welfare organizations offer body-safety education for young children. One example is the Stand Up and ROAR program for ages 4–8, which teaches body safety and how to report abuse. ROAR stands for:

- Remember — privates are private.
- Okay to say no.
- Always talk about secrets.
- Raise your voice and tell someone.

Parents and school staff should contact their local Child Advocacy Center to ask about available programs; many are free and designed to make learning empowering and age-appropriate.

How to respond when a child tells you — a parent script

- Pause, breathe, and give full attention. Get down to their eye level.
- **Believe and affirm:** "Thank you for telling me. I believe you."
- **Reassure safety:** "You are safe with me."
- **Offer an open invitation:** "Can you tell me what happened?" or "Can you show me where?" (If the child refuses, do not push).

- **Say next steps:** "I'm going to keep you safe and get help."
- **Avoid interrogation:** do not ask for graphic details, ask "why," or suggest answers.
- **Preserve evidence:** do not bathe the child or change bedding/clothing if abuse may have occurred; seek medical attention promptly.
- Report immediately to child protective services and law enforcement; follow mandated-reporting laws.

Role-play practice (short, realistic drills)

- **Preschool:** Practice stepping away and finding a trusted adult after saying, "No. Stop. I'll tell Mom."
- **Elementary:** Practice saying, "Please stop. Don't touch my chest. I'm going to tell my teacher."
- **Teen:** Rehearse, "I'm not comfortable. We're done. I need to go," and practice texting a preset contact or using the family safety word.

Institutional safeguards every parent should demand

- Background checks and training for all staff and volunteers.
- Two-adult rule: avoid closed-door one-on-one contact with minors; meetings should be visible and supervised.
- Written, posted child-protection policies and external oversight — no internal-only investigations.
- Mandatory reporting protocols and training on grooming, boundaries, and anatomy.

Red flags in adults

- Insistence on private time alone with a child.
- Requests for secrecy or "our little secret."

- Gifts tied to expectations or silence.
- Persistent boundary testing (tickles, extended hugs, inappropriate comments).
- Attempts to undermine parents or encourage secrecy.

Signs in children that something may be wrong

- Sudden withdrawal, nightmares, bedwetting, or increased anxiety.
- Sexualized behavior beyond developmental norms or use of adult sexual language.
- Unexplained injuries or refusal to change for gym/swim.
- Decline in school performance or social isolation.
- Reluctance to be around a specific adult or to attend certain activities.

Why clarity matters

Euphemisms obscure what happened, slow investigations, and retraumatize children. Teaching anatomically correct names is an evidence-backed intervention: it preserves clarity, speeds help and strengthens accountability. A child who can say, "Uncle Billy touched my vulva," gives professionals the precise information they need to act quickly and protect them.

Call to action

- Teach anatomical names matter-of-factly.
- Model asking permission before touching.
- Honor every "no."
- Role-play responses with children.
- Demand visible one-on-one interactions and institutional safeguards.
- Report concerns without hesitation.

If we change our behavior now, we give children the far greater gift of bodily autonomy. When a child speaks, listen, believe, and act. That clarity can be the difference between confusion and protection — and it can save a life.

CHAPTER NOTES:

Chapter 17

Predators in Your Own Home-Family, Friends, and Trusted People

This chapter discusses sexual abuse and investigative procedures. If someone is in immediate danger, call emergency services now.

The hardest truth to hold is this: too often the person who should be safest at the kitchen table is the one who is most dangerous. When predators are family members, siblings, neighbors, coaches, clergy, or trusted family friends, the harm arrives wrapped in routine—dinner invitations, holiday gatherings, babysitting favors, rides to practice—so it is easy to tell yourself, "Not our house, not our people." That reassurance can let abuse continue. The betrayal is not only sexual or physical; it is an erosion of the basic contract of care that families rely on, and that is what makes domestic predators uniquely cruel and effective at hiding in plain sight.

Non-stranger predators exploit the architecture of your life: they know schedules, blind spots, and who will resist believing a claim against them. Grooming is deliberate: it begins with small, seemingly benign breaches—private jokes, extra attention, "special" time— and escalates by rewarding secrecy, isolating the child, and normalizing boundary crossing. A gift, a favor, or a private ride home can be the currency that buys silence. Gaslighting follows doubts about memory, blame directed at the survivor, or warnings that "telling will break the family." These patterns are not accidental. They are the plan, and they move slowly because slow gives the abuser power.

Scenes that show how grooming looks in everyday life:

Scene one (relative): A young boy lights up every Sunday when his uncle arrives with comics and candy. At first it is stories on the couch and a secret handshake; then the adult asks for the door closed "so we can hear the story better," then insists the boy mustn't tell because "grown-ups won't understand." When the boy finally says he's uncomfortable, he's dismissed and warned that telling will make the family angry. The family alternates between denial and pressured loyalty; the man keeps coming. Years later the boy realizes love was used as a lock—and telling one believing teacher begins the work of accountability.

Scene two (neighbor/coach): A high-school girl's neighbor—father of a teammate—starts by driving her to games and taking "fun" photos. Compliments become private texts; "You could trust me" becomes a demand to delete messages and keep secrets. When she recoils, he reminds her of how much he's helped and frames kindness as leverage. A cousin eventually sees a text and tells her she deserves better. She tells an aunt who believes, preserves evidence, and connects her with a counselor and an advocate. Professionals intervene: the man is removed from roles around children.

Short example (cousin): Jamie was eight when an older cousin, Max, began giving extra snacks, late nights, and a secret handshake. Secrecy became approval. One night Max crossed physical boundaries and warned Jamie not to tell, framing silence as loyalty. This example illustrates the same grooming arc in a different family role.

These scenes are not horror stories meant to shock—they are everyday scripts parents can miss. Parents often trust what ease and routine teach them: a name at the dinner table feels safe. That assumption undermines the urgency to interrupt grooming. You do not have to be suspicious of everyone; you need to be clear-eyed about behaviors that are red flags.

Red flags to watch for:

- Persistent private time with a child (closed doors, "special" privileges).
- Insistence on secrecy: "It's our secret," requests to delete messages.
- Inappropriate physical contact or sexualized talk.
- Requests for private photos, account passwords, or gifts that solicit silence.
- Attempts to isolate a child from friends or other adults, or to undermine caregivers.

If you suspect abuse: immediate practical steps:

If there is imminent danger, call emergency services. Move the child to a safe place if you can without escalating risk. Preserve potential evidence: do not launder clothing, change bedding, or delete messages. Take screenshots from a safe device and back them up; keep originals intact where possible. Write contemporaneous notes: dates, times, exact words, and who else was present. Seek medical attention promptly; a forensic medical exam can address injuries, offer emergency contraception and STI testing, and preserve evidence. You do not have to file a police report to receive medical care.

How you respond when someone discloses:

How you respond matters more than what you fear you'll uncover. If a child or adult tells you something, do these things:

- Believe them and thank them for telling you.
- Say clearly: "You did nothing wrong." Avoid interrogation: do not demand a graphic retelling, do not ask "why," and do not express blame.
- Do not confront the suspected abuser alone—this can increase danger and destroy evidence.
- Contact a trained advocate, child-protective services, or law enforcement for immediate guidance. Advocates can help create a safety plan, preserve evidence, and explain reporting options without pressuring you.

Immediate checklist (do these first):

- If there is immediate danger, call emergency services now.
- Get the child to a safe place with a trusted adult who will believe and protect them.
- Do not force a graphic account. Do not wash clothing or discard devices that may contain evidence.
- Preserve texts, photos, and messages: take screenshots from a separate device and back them up. Keep originals when safe.
- Contact a sexual-assault/child-advocate hotline for immediate guidance and a local Sexual Assault Nurse examiner (SANE)/forensic exam location.
- Document: date/time, what was said, who was present (write it down immediately and store securely).

Scripts — say these aloud, word for word if you need to.

If a child discloses to you (parent/caregiver):

"I'm so glad you told me. Thank you for telling me — I believe you. You did nothing wrong. I'm going to keep you safe. I don't need all the details right now. Can you tell me, in your own words, what happened? If you can't say it now, that's okay — you can tell me later. I'm going to call someone who can help us keep you safe and get care. Do you want [name of trusted adult] with us right now?"

Why these lines work: They validate, remove blame, avoid interrogation, and give the child an immediate protection plan.

Phone script for advocates or hotlines:

"Hello — my name is [your name]. I have a concern about possible sexual abuse of [child's name], age [age], by [relationship to child]. I need immediate guidance on safety planning, evidence preservation, and local SANE/forensic exam options. Can you stay on the phone with me while I make a safety plan? I also need information about mandatory reporting and services for caregivers."

Ask the advocate:

- "What are the immediate steps we should take to keep the child safe?"
- "Where is the nearest forensic exam (SANE) location, and what will they do?"
- "Can you connect me to local counseling and legal help?"

Digital and financial control — practical steps

- Change passwords from a secure device and enable two-factor authentication.
- Archive abusive communications while keeping originals intact. If you suspect remote monitoring of devices, power them down and seek professional help.
- If someone controls household finances, document transactions and seek legal advice about emergency financial protections and independent access to funds.

Accountability, healing, and family repair

When children are harmed by family, the fallout is complex: loyalties fracture, reputations are defended, and some relatives may protect the abuser. Protecting a child is not betrayal—it is survival. True accountability requires transparent investigation, professional oversight, and enforceable boundaries: temporary separation, supervised visits, or legal restrictions when necessary—before any discussion of reconciliation.

Healing is slow and must center the survivor. Immediate needs are safety and medical care; next are validation and trauma-informed therapy. Family repair, if ever appropriate, comes only after sustained accountability, professional mediation, and a track record of consistent, boundary-respecting behavior. Practical rituals of safety— shared visible calendars, no one-on-one closed-door time with children, financial transparency—help rebuild trust.

A personal note

You are not alone. Although this is not a firsthand account, years of work in child welfare make clear how betrayal within families causes deep harm. Silence enables abuse; timely, careful intervention can prevent further damage. Heed your instincts, document concerns precisely, and seek medical, legal, and advocacy support right away. Prioritize safety over reputation.

Call to action — quick decisions to make now:

Do not wait for certainty to act. If a single moment in your home rings wrong, treat it as the beginning of a protective response, not a family rumor to be smoothed over. Decide now who can take a child immediately if needed, where you will go, and which advocate or medical center you will call. Keep this page reachable and share it with other adults who care for your children. Belief, documentation, medical care, and outside support stop predators who are allowed at the kitchen table.

CHAPTER NOTES:

Chapter 18

The Role of Schools and Communities

There is a quiet courage in the daily work of classrooms and playgrounds, and much of the safety children need is born from the steady presence of teachers, counselors, coaches, and staff who show up, notice, and hold space for young people. As educators, you are often the first safe person a child encounters outside the family: the steady voice in the hallway, the patient adult at dismissal, the teacher who remembers a child's favorite book. This chapter honors that work and speaks directly to the strengths and realities of school life, offering practical ways to partner with families and communities while protecting your own wellbeing.

Partnering with families starts from a place of mutual respect and clear communication. Invite parents into the life of the school through open conversations about safety expectations, routines, and the support the school offers. Establish regular, predictable channels for updates— whether through parent-teacher meetings, brief check-ins after school events, or collaborative safety committees—so concerns do not build in silence. When a worry arises about a child, a collaborative approach that shares observations, listens to context, and focuses on the child's needs helps build trust and speeds meaningful action. For teachers, that might mean documenting changes in behavior, alerting a counselor or student-support team early, and gently guiding parents to resources without assuming blame. When schools and families truly partner, children gain consistency and adults gain allies.

Recognizing what a safe environment looks like goes beyond appearances to the policies and daily practices that protect and empower students. Safe schools are characterized by clear child-protection policies, consistent supervision, a culture of respectful boundaries, and staff trained to respond with compassion and competence when a child discloses distress. Teachers can be catalysts for these practices by modeling respectful interactions, insisting on transparent procedures for reporting concerns, and advocating for professional development in trauma-informed approaches. If you see gaps—unclear reporting channels, inconsistent supervision during transitions, or disciplinary practices that isolate students—advocating for change can begin with data and small, concrete proposals: a request for staff training, a suggestion for a written protocol, or an invitation to pilot restorative circles. Framing requests around student safety and learning helps move conversations from defensiveness to action.

Building support networks with other parents and community members strengthens the protective web around children while easing the burden on any single adult. Teachers can help create or nurture parent networks that share practical support—carpooling, after-school supervision, or check-ins for students who frequently miss school—and also serve as forums for constructive advocacy. Equally important are the professional support networks among educators: peer consultation groups, mentoring relationships, and staff wellness teams that allow teachers to debrief difficult incidents, coordinate responses, and avoid isolation. Community partners—local health services, youth programs, faith groups, and social services—can extend capacity when schools coordinate with them. When staff work together with families and local organizations, the result is not only safer school settings but a stronger, shared responsibility for children's wellbeing.

Understanding legal protections and reporting mechanisms can feel intimidating, but knowledge is a powerful tool that protects both students and staff. Many school staff are designated as mandatory reporters and are required to report reasonable suspicions of abuse or neglect; knowing your school's internal procedures as well as local reporting channels helps you act confidently and appropriately. Keep careful, factual documentation—dates, observable behaviors, direct quotations, who was informed—so that concerns can be clearly communicated to counselors, administrators, or child-protective services when necessary. It's also important to recognize the difference between an internal support response and a formal investigation, and to work with your administration to ensure that any actions taken prioritize the child's safety, dignity, and privacy. If you fear potential repercussions from reporting, seek guidance from your school's designated safeguarding lead or legal counsel; you are protected by policies that exist to uphold student safety.

The emotional labor of protecting children is real, and teachers deserve support in carrying it. Responding to disclosures or managing complex family situations can stir anxiety, grief, or moral distress; schools that normalize debriefing, provide access to counseling, and allow time for staff to process difficult events help sustain their teams. Advocate for regular, trauma-informed training that includes not only how to spot signs of harm but also how to respond in ways that minimize re-traumatization and preserve classroom stability. Small practices—brief check-ins among colleagues, shared expectations about who handles disclosures during class time, and clear escalation pathways—reduce the cognitive load on individual teachers and ensure students receive coordinated care.

Finally, remember that change is often incremental and that your everyday acts of care matter enormously. Speak up when policies fall short, celebrate small wins when a risky situation is averted, and lean on your colleagues when a case becomes heavy. Use your voice for systems-level improvements—safer supervision practices, clearer reporting pathways, restorative discipline options—but also give yourself permission to seek help and set boundaries so you can keep doing this vital work effectively.

Your commitment shapes the lives of children in ways that are profound and lasting; the community and the school are stronger because of the care you bring each day.

CHAPTER NOTES:

Chapter 19

Coping with Loss and Trauma

Children who experience grief or trauma live in two worlds at once: the ordinary world of school, snacks, playdates, and homework, and an interior world that can feel unpredictable, frightening, and isolating

Grief opens doors we don't always see. When a family is grieving, both the parent and the child become more vulnerable. What does this have to do with predators? A grieving parent may be overwhelmed, exhausted, or simply trying to hold everything together — and in that space, subtle changes in a child's behavior can be easy to miss. Children experiencing loss may seek comfort, reassurance, or connection elsewhere, creating emotional gaps that predators are skilled at stepping into. It is not a failure of love — it is the reality of grief. Awareness is what closes the cracks before someone else tries to slip through them.

Unlike adults, who often have language and life experience to organize feelings into a coherent story, children communicate through behavior, play, somatic complaints, and sudden mood shifts. A toddler may return to bedwetting and clinginess after a caregiver dies; a seven-year-old may insist the loss is temporary and ask the same question repeatedly; a thirteen-year-old may withdraw, prioritize new friendships, or act out aggressively; and a teen may numb with substances or risky behavior while insisting they are "fine." These behaviors are not mischief or stubbornness; they are attempts to make sense of a rupture in safety and to regain control in developmentally meaningful ways. Recognizing that grief and trauma look different at different ages is the first step toward responding in ways that soothe rather than silence a child's suffering.

Children's grief reactions are shaped by developmental stage, the relationship to the person lost, the circumstances of the death or trauma, and adults' responses. Very young children have a limited concept of permanence and may expect a return or believe they caused the event; for them, repetition and reassurance matter. School-age children begin to grasp finality but often retain magical thinking and intense guilt; they worry about who will care for them and may express grief through physical complaints or regression. Adolescents can understand permanence but may feel overwhelmed by complex emotions, existential questions, and social pressures; they may oscillate between wanting privacy and craving connection. Traumatic loss — sudden, violent, or preventable deaths, or losses within contexts of chronic stress, displacement, or abuse — can compound grief with fear, hypervigilance, intrusive memories, and avoidance. Trauma can disrupt a child's sense of safety in body and environment and fracture trust in adults who are supposed to protect them. For many children, the core struggle is not only missing the person who died but relearning how to feel safe enough to play, learn, and imagine a future.

How adults respond will shape how a child weathers this storm. The most healing responses are simple and steady: honest, age-appropriate language; calm presence; and repeated reassurance that the child is not to blame and that caregivers will protect and support them. Avoid euphemisms that can be misunderstood — say "died" instead of "went to sleep." Answer questions simply and be prepared to answer some of them many times. Name feelings aloud: "You look sad; I feel sad too," models emotional literacy and validates the child's experience without pathologizing it. Use play, drawing, storytelling, and role-play with younger children; these are their natural languages.

Encourage school-age children to write letters, keep memory boxes, or create rituals that honor the person who died. For teens, offer privacy and respect but keep lines of communication open; invite them into decisions about memorials or family routines to restore agency.

Routines and predictability are powerful healing tools. During grief, the world can feel chaotic; consistent mealtimes, bedtimes, school attendance, and caregiver transitions create a scaffold of safety. Rituals of remembrance — lighting a candle on important dates, making a scrapbook, or planting a tree — give grief a place in daily life and help children hold memories without being consumed by them. Encourage age-appropriate roles that let children contribute, whether setting the table, reading to a younger sibling, or helping plan a family memory event. These responsibilities restore competence and counter helplessness. At the same time, protect children from adult responsibilities such as managing finances or mediating family conflicts; undue burden can entrench anxiety and impede healthy development.

Behavioral changes are common and should be met with curiosity rather than punishment. A child acting out at school may be signaling internal distress rather than willful defiance. Teachers and school counselors can be invaluable partners, providing stability, monitoring attention and learning, and offering short-term accommodations while a child adjusts. Collaborate with schools on plans for brief breaks, reduced homework when needed, or identified safe adults the child can go to during overwhelming moments.

Watch for somatic symptoms — headaches, stomachaches, appetite or sleep changes — which often express distress and can be dismissed as "just nerves." If these physical symptoms persist or worsen, seek pediatric evaluation; pediatricians can assess the interplay between emotional stress and bodily symptoms and recommend appropriate care.

Knowing when to seek professional help is vital. Most children gradually adjust with supportive caregiving and community resources, but seek evaluation when distress persists beyond several weeks to months and significantly interferes with daily functioning; when intense fear, intrusive memories, severe nightmares, avoidance of places or people related to the trauma, or marked behavior changes (aggression, self-harm, substance use) appear; when developmental regression does not resolve; or when there are signs of severe depression or suicidal ideation.

Early intervention often prevents symptom entrenchment. Effective treatments for trauma and complicated grief in children are trauma-informed and developmentally sensitive: trauma-focused cognitive behavioral therapy (TF-CBT) uses gradual exposure, coping skills, and caregiver involvement to process traumatic memories safely; play therapy provides a nonverbal avenue for younger children; eye movement desensitization and reprocessing therapy (EMDR) has adapted protocols for some children and adolescents; family therapy can repair communication ruptures and strengthen caregiving; and, in certain cases, medication may be considered alongside therapy under psychiatric guidance. The best plans involve caregivers as partners, teaching co-regulation strategies and ways to support the child between sessions.

Caregivers' emotional states profoundly influence a child's recovery. Children read cues from adults' tones, facial expressions, and consistency; an overwhelmed or avoidant caregiver may unintentionally transmit anxiety or shame. Caregivers need permission to grieve and to seek their own support – through friends, family, peer bereavement groups, or therapy — because a regulated, supported caregiver is the greatest buffer against long-term harm.

Self-care for caregivers does not require grand gestures. It can mean attending to basic needs like sleep and nutrition, scheduling short breaks, accepting practical help, and creating predictable moments of recreation. It also includes setting boundaries with well-meaning but intrusive people and protecting children from media that sensationalizes the trauma. When financial or housing instability strains family resources, connect with community services; alleviating chronic stressors creates space for emotional work.

Building resilience in families is an active, relational process rather than an innate trait. Resilience grows from stable, nurturing relationships; clear, compassionate communication; consistent routines; opportunities for children to exercise agency and competence; and access to social supports. Families can practice emotional regulation together by naming feelings out loud, modeling coping skills, and rehearsing calming strategies such as slow breathing, grounding (noting sensory details in the present), or brief movement breaks.

Encourage activities that foster connection and identity beyond the loss: joining a club, volunteering, or cultivating artistic or athletic pursuits that allow children to experience mastery and joy. Celebrate small progress and normalize setbacks; recovery is rarely linear, and anniversaries, transitions, or reminders can trigger renewed waves of grief even years later.

Cultural, spiritual, and familial contexts shape mourning and meaning making. Rituals that honor the deceased can be stabilizing — religious services, family storytelling, cooking favorite meals, or visits to a special place. Respect children's cultural and spiritual expressions and include them in decisions about rituals according to age and preference. Be mindful that cultural stigma about mental health can create barriers to seeking therapy; culturally responsive clinicians and community advocates can bridge this gap and help families find acceptable forms of support.

A long-term perspective matters. Children may appear to adapt well and then exhibit delayed reactions months or years later — during puberty, graduations, first romantic relationships, or other milestones that stir questions about identity and belonging. Keep lines of communication open across time, check in on anniversaries and transitions, and watch for changes in friendships, school performance, or mood. Normalizing the ebb and flow of grief — acknowledging that certain times will be harder — allows families to plan supportive responses ahead of time.

Finally, humility and gentleness are important when supporting grieving children. There is no perfect script, and well-intentioned adults sometimes say the wrong thing. What matters most is presence: showing up, listening without rushing to fix, validating feelings, and creating reliable structures that make a child feel safe. When additional help is needed, reaching out early to mental-health professionals, school supports, and community resources increases the chances of recovery and reduces the risk of long-term impairment. Grief and trauma change children, but with sensitive caregiving, predictable routines, culturally attuned rituals, and timely professional support, children can integrate their losses into lives that remain rich with learning, relationships, and hope.

Don't Disappear When Grief Hits

When Jacob died in 2012, I made choices that, though unintentional, shaped my children's mental health and created vulnerabilities I didn't see. My inability to deal with the loss trickled down to my children not being able to deal with the loss.

When Jarred died in 2017, those earlier wounds mattered — it created a vulnerability that led him down a path of destruction. I don't want anyone else to make the same mistakes I did.

Final note: Grief is messy and imperfect. You will stumble. The difference is this: stay present, document what you notice, and ask for help early. Don't do what I did.

Onward.

CHAPTER NOTES:

Chapter 20

Empowering Children for Safety

Empowering children for safety requires treating safety as a dynamic set of competencies—awareness, judgment, communication, and action—that adults intentionally teach, model, and reinforce. At its heart this work is an act of respect: believing children can learn to read situations, trust their instincts, and take steps to protect themselves and others. When safety education moves beyond rote rules and into skill-building, rehearsal, leadership opportunities, and real-world problem solving, children do more than memorize what to do; they internalize ways of thinking that allow them to act calmly and confidently when it matters most.

Teaching self-awareness and intuition starts with the simple practice of helping children notice inner signals and external clues. For very young children, this looks like naming physical sensations—warm cheeks, a racing heart, a tight stomach—and connecting them to emotions such as worry, fear, or discomfort. With elementary-age children, introduce short mindfulness-style check-ins: "What do you notice in your body right now?" or "Where do you feel the 'uh-oh' feeling?" For older youth, teach them to triangulate between physical cues, emotional responses, and contextual information: who is involved, what is expected, and what seems out of alignment. Emphasize that intuition is not supernatural, but a pattern-recognition skill built from experience. Encourage children to report feelings without fear of being dismissed so their early warnings are consistently taken seriously by trusted adults.

Practice makes intuition practical. Short, repeated activities—such as a "body map" where children draw where they feel different emotions, or a daily two-minute noticing game during drop-off—build habit. Use stories and media literacy to analyze characters' decisions: ask, "What clues would make you trust or not trust that person?" and model how adults check their own instincts. Teach a simple internal checklist children can use in any setting: pause, name the feeling, look around, choose one safe action. Reinforce that safety is multi-layered: physical escape routes, words to assert boundaries, and the social practice of telling a trusted adult are all valid and often complementary responses.

Role-playing bridges awareness and action by creating low-stakes opportunities to rehearse real responses. Design scenarios that mirror children's daily routines—saying no to uncomfortable touch, refusing peer pressure, losing sight of a caregiver, encountering a stranger with an urgent request, or dealing with online contact that feels inappropriate. Begin with short, scaffolded exercises: adults model a confident tone and posture, children repeat lines like "I don't like that" or "No, thank you," and then practice moving to a safe place or calling a buddy. Gradually increase complexity by introducing ambiguity and pressure: a friendly-sounding adult who insists, a popular classmate pushing for a secret, or a confusing instruction from an authority figure. After each enactment, debrief with open, nonjudgmental questions—what you noticed, what helped you feel safe, what could you try differently—and celebrate attempts, resilience, and creativity.

Practical role-play scripts can anchor skills. For example, a simple script for a child approached by an adult offering candy: child steps back, uses firm voice to say "No, thank you," turns to a nearby adult and states, "I need help," and moves toward a safe adult or public space. For older children, practice assertive boundary language that still preserves respect: "I don't feel comfortable with that. Please stop." Incorporate safe escape strategies—running to a group setting, finding a shopkeeper, or using a prearranged code word with a caregiver. Use props, visual cues, and peer actors to increase realism, and always debrief to normalize that nervousness is expected and that trying is the point.

Encouraging leadership and peer support amplifies safety because children often listen to and emulate one another. Create structured roles—safety buddies, crossing guards, classroom safety captains—that rotate so every child experiences responsibility. Pair older and younger children in mentorships where older peers teach boundary-setting games or model walking home in pairs. Teach specific peer-intervention language that is simple and safe: "Let's go," "That makes me uncomfortable," or "We don't do that here." Encourage bystander intervention in developmentally appropriate ways—disrupting a risky interaction by creating noise and presence, seeking adult help, or physically removing a friend from a concerning situation when it is safe to do so. Reinforce that asking for help and stepping in for others are leadership skills, not tattling, and celebrate community norms where watching out for one another is valued.

Leadership can also be nurtured through projects: safety-themed drama performances, student-created safety maps of school grounds, or peer-led workshops on digital privacy. These projects let children own the content and language of safety, which increases uptake. For communities and schools, building a culture of shared responsibility reduces isolation; when safety is communal, the burden doesn't rest solely on a child to manage risk.

Helping children develop problem-solving skills equips them to generate options rather than feeling trapped by a single "right" choice. Teach age-appropriate frameworks: for preschoolers, a three-step plan—see it, say it, go to an adult; for school-age children, a four-step process—identify the problem, brainstorm at least three responses, choose the safest, and check what happens; for adolescents, add reflection and contingency planning, asking "If this doesn't work, what will I try next?" Use guided brainstorming to expand thinking beyond flight or freeze responses—making noise, creating a distraction, enlisting peers, or using technology to call for help may all be viable. Practice evaluating risks: what are the likely consequences of each option, who can help, and which actions keep your body and dignity safe?

Encourage creative thinking through games that reward multiple solutions. Pose hypothetical dilemmas and let teams come up with as many safe responses as they can, scoring points for originality and feasibility. Use reflective exercises after incidents—real or practiced—so children learn to evaluate outcomes and revise plans. Teach concrete decision tools such as "STOP" (Stop, Think, Observe, Plan) or "PAUSE" (Pause, Assess, Use your voice, Seek help), choosing language that fits the age and cultural context of the child.

Implementation is where good intentions become results. Embed safety learning in routines: morning check-ins that include a safety question, classroom stories that highlight boundary-respecting behavior, and weekly micro-practices of role-play. Train caregivers and staff in consistent responses so children learn that disclosures are met with calm, action, and confidentiality when appropriate. Create clear reporting systems and visible, trusted adults in schools and communities—everyone should know who they can turn to. For families, provide simple home practices: a family safety plan with trusted adults and meeting places, a code word for emergencies, and regular conversations that normalize asking for help.

Cultural responsiveness and trauma-informed practice are essential. Recognize that children's experiences and the norms around autonomy and boundaries vary widely; adapt language and role-plays so they resonate with family values and community expectations. Use trauma-informed approaches: avoid re-traumatizing detail, emphasize choice and agency, and prioritize emotional safety. For children who have experienced harm, focus on rebuilding trust through predictable routines, gradual skill-building, and collaboration with mental health professionals when needed.

Measuring impact keeps programs honest and adaptive. Track observable behaviors—use of assertive language, reliance on buddy systems, prompt reporting of concerning events—rather than relying solely on knowledge checks. Solicit children's own feedback: what feels helpful? what feels scary? and what would make safety practices more useful in their lives? Share successes and lessons learned with families and staff to build momentum and adjust curriculum to real-world needs.

Address common adult worries head-on. Some caregivers fear that teaching children about danger will create anxiety. Research and practice show that age-appropriate, skill-based safety education decreases fear and increases confidence because it gives children concrete tools and supportive adults who listen. Emphasize empowerment over alarm: the goal is to increase competence and connection, not to scare.

Finally, the most powerful safety lessons come from modeling. Adults who demonstrate calm decision-making, clear boundary-setting, and respectful assertion teach children more than any lesson plan. When caregivers promptly act on children's concerns, follow through on safety plans, and invite children into problem-solving conversations, they signal that safety is a shared responsibility and that children's voices matter.

Empowering children for safety is both a daily practice and a long-term commitment. It asks adults to build systems that honor intuition, create plentiful rehearsal opportunities, cultivate peer leadership, and teach problem-solving that anticipates multiple paths to safety. When these elements come together—habits of noticing, practiced responses, a culture of mutual support, and flexible thinking—children grow not into people who live in fear, but into confident agents who can navigate risk with judgment, voice, and community behind them.

CHAPTER NOTES:

Chapter 21

AI, Sexting and Sextortion

This chapter is not background noise—you need to read it as if someone has kicked down your front door. A new epidemic moves through places we used to think private: the bedroom, the direct message, the group chat. Sexting, sextortion, and artificial intelligence have fused into a predator's perfect storm.

What began as adolescent experimentation— flirtatious snaps, private jokes, the naïve intimacy of teens— has been weaponized into industrial-scale humiliation. A single impulsive photo is no longer a reversible mistake; it can become a permanent weapon. Images can be copied, altered, and, with generative AI, entirely fabricated. Algorithms can erase clothing, swap faces, stitch body parts together, and manufacture "proof" that never existed. A photo taken in confidence can be turned into a lifeline for blackmail, shared across countless platforms, and remixed into a viral lie.

Case Study: Payton

Payton was a well-liked high school athlete — confident, outgoing, and surrounded by friends. One afternoon, he received a message from a girl his age on social media. Her profile appeared normal, with casual photos, followers from nearby schools, and shared interests, so Payton accepted her friend request. Their conversation started casually, talking about sports, music, and classes. She seemed friendly and interested in him, and the attention felt flattering.

After a few days of messaging, she asked what he looked like "today" and encouraged him to send a picture. Wanting to keep things light, Payton sent a fully appropriate photo of himself from the chest up. Within minutes, everything changed. The account holder used AI image manipulation to alter the photo into a nude image. She then sent the edited picture back to Payton with a threat: if he didn't send Xbox gift cards and comply with her ongoing demands, she would distribute the fake image to his school, his teammates, and his family.

Payton panicked. Even though *he had done nothing wrong*, the fear of humiliation and disbelief caused him to shut down. He didn't tell his friends or his coach. He stopped sleeping, avoided practice, and became withdrawn. His parents noticed the dramatic change and asked gentle, direct questions. Only then did Payton disclose what was happening.

Because he told an adult, the situation was stopped quickly. Law enforcement was contacted, his accounts were secured, and he received support in navigating the emotional fallout. The "girl" he had been speaking to was not a peer — it was an adult predator using a manufactured identity to groom and extort teens online

Hear this clearly: in the digital world, there is no true privacy. Everything done online or on cell phones is effectively public and permanent. Messages that vanish for a moment can be saved, screenshotted, and re-uploaded; ephemeral apps create a false sense of safety but leave emotional and legal wreckage when images reappear. The databases of the internet are not kind—they replicate, archive, and resurface. Search engines, image caches, reposts, and anonymous forums mean that once something exists digitally, it can live forever.

Even when an image is removed, fragments and rumors remain cached copies, screenshots in private chats, whispers in school hallways. The permanence of the internet means the humiliation can follow a child into college applications, job interviews, and intimate relationships for years to come.

This is not rare or abstract. Child protection groups and internet safety organizations are seeing sharp increases in AI-generated sexual content and targeted sextortion against minors. Attackers begin with ordinary contact—a compliment, a "trade pics?" request, a manipulated screenshot that appears to come from a friend—and escalate into organized coercion.

Threats to distribute images can quickly turn to demands for money, more images, or sexual acts. The terror of "it will be everywhere" drives kids into silence; they fear the long-term social exile that a viral image creates. Predators fine-tune their tactics: they research social networks, learn names of siblings and teachers, and tailor threats so they feel imminent and inescapable. They exploit the speed and anonymity of the internet to move from flirtation to blackmail in hours.

The human cost is devastating. Beyond immediate shame, victims suffer lasting trauma: anxiety, insomnia, withdrawal, self-harm, and a crushing sense of being exposed that reshapes identity. In the worst tragedies, teenagers have taken their own lives after images—real or fabricated—were circulated widely. Even when content is proven fake, the stigma lingers. Rumors spread faster than facts, and reputations, scholarship opportunities, and future prospects can be destroyed in the space of a morning. Parents who believed their worst fear was "an embarrassing photo" face losses that cannot be repaired with apologies. A child's ability to trust, to form relationships, to feel safe in school—these are eroded by a single digital moment.

The systems meant to protect children are struggling to keep up. Perpetrators exploit encrypted platforms, burner accounts, disappearing messages, and AI tools that erase metadata and create plausible deniability. Platforms are overwhelmed by volume and often slow to act on sophisticated synthetic media. Law enforcement units may lack the resources or training to chase cross-border digital crimes quickly. That waiting period—minutes, hours, days—can be the difference between a contained scare and a life-altering catastrophe.

Extortionists demand untraceable payments; families, terrified of public shame, sometimes comply—and too often the payment does not stop the abuse. This transactional model reveals a grim truth: sextortion is organized criminality, run like a business, preying on fear and social vulnerability.

So, what must parents do? This is not a checklist to soothe guilt; it is a blueprint for urgent action. First, accept the hard fact: everything your child does online is potentially public and permanent. Treat devices and accounts with the same seriousness as you would treat the house keys. Require phones to be charged in communal spaces overnight. Know every app on your child's devices and how those apps work—especially anonymity features, disappearing messages, and hidden chats. Use two-factor authentication, secure routers, and age-appropriate parental controls. Regularly review friend lists, usernames, and privacy settings together. Don't let "they'll hate me" stop you; explain that safety sometimes looks like limits.

Teach concrete rules without moralizing: under no circumstances should they send intimate images. Make it unequivocal that they will never be punished if they come to you after a mistake. Normalize conversations about consent, manipulation, and coercion so that a child feels safe telling the truth. Give them language for refusal and de-escalation—how to say no, how to block and report, and how to preserve evidence if threatened: screenshots, usernames, timestamps, and URLs. Preserve evidence safely and promptly: use multiple screenshots, note the context, and store copies offline.

If your child reports sextortion, your reaction will shape the outcome. Do not respond with shame or rage. React calmly, protectively, and immediately. Report the content to the platform and demand takedown; document your reports. Contact law enforcement—digital extortion is a crime and should be treated as such. Notify school officials and insist on supportive, not punitive, responses. Seek mental health support right away: a child's withdrawal, talk of humiliation, or expressions of hopelessness demand immediate professional attention. Shame delays lifesaving action.

Push for systemic accountability. Demand better tools and faster takedowns from platforms. Insist that schools adopt victim-focused policies and education programs that teach digital literacy, consent, and bystander intervention. Advocate for law enforcement resources to investigate cross-jurisdictional digital crimes. This epidemic is larger than any one family; it requires coordinated public pressure to change norms and infrastructure.

Finally, change your mindset from passive supervision to active guardianship without stifling autonomy. Educate, monitor, and rehearse responses. Role-play scenarios so children know what to say and do if pressured. Build a clear family protocol for an incident— who you contact, where evidence is stored, and how to access mental health support. Remember: prevention is both technological and emotional. Equip your child with practical security, and with the confidence to come to you.

Everything done online or on cell phones is effectively public and permanent. That reality should terrify and mobilize you. Don't accept "kids will be kids." One cropped selfie, one flattering headshot, one careless reply can become permanent collateral. Wake up, watch, talk, and act now. The cost of complacency is too high: reputations wrecked, futures narrowed, and in too many heartbreaking cases, lives ended. Protect your child with the urgency this crisis demands.

Call to Action

This is not the moment to hope your child will "figure it out" or that danger will look obvious when it appears. Predators are counting on good parents being busy, trusting, polite, and hesitant to ask uncomfortable questions. Do not give them that advantage. From this point forward, make it your responsibility to *actively* know who your child is talking to, what platforms they are using, and what is happening in their emotional world. Sit down with your child and ask — plainly, without judgment — if anyone has ever made them feel uncomfortable, pressured them, asked for photos, tried to keep secrets, or made them feel like something couldn't be shared at home. Do not wait for them to bring it to you. Most won't. They are afraid of getting in trouble, being embarrassed, or not being believed.

Create a home where the truth can be spoken, the very first time something feels wrong. Establish clear boundaries around phones, gaming, privacy, sleepovers, transportation, and online communication — and enforce them. Know the adults and older teens who have access to your child. Trust your instincts when something feels off, and act immediately. If something has happened, do not minimize it, dismiss it, or handle it privately. Protect your child, document what you learn, and report to the proper authorities.

Your child needs you to be alert, involved, and unafraid to be the parent who stands between them and harm. Do not trade their safety for social comfort, fear of conflict, or the hope that "it won't happen here." It can. It has. It will — unless you choose to see, to ask, and to act. Your voice, your presence, and your willingness to step in could be the very thing that saves your child's life.

CHAPTER NOTES:

Chapter 22

Lockdown & Limits: How to Protect Kids Devices

Locking down devices is not about erecting walls of control or spying on young people; it's about establishing clear, humane boundaries that protect developing minds, preserve family connection, and teach the skills children will need to navigate a digital world. Parental controls are the scaffolding for those boundaries—tools that, when used with intention, reduce temptation, limit exposure to harmful content, and make the invisible architecture of the internet visible and manageable for caregivers. Built-in utilities like Apple's Screen Time and Google's Family Link, complemented by router-level controls or dedicated family-security appliances, let you set time limits, filter web content, prevent unwanted purchases, and create separate child accounts.

Use these features not as punitive levers but as graduated supports: tighter restrictions for young children, more autonomy paired with oversight for adolescents. Keep administrative credentials secure, document why each rule exists, and schedule periodic reviews so settings evolve with your child's maturity rather than becoming permanent blunt instruments.

"No phone zones" are simple, high-impact practices that protect sleep, sustain attention, and reclaim presence in the home. Decide together—when possible—on physical and temporal boundaries: the kitchen table during meals, bedrooms, bathrooms, family conversations, and study times can all be sanctified as device-free. Normalize the ritual of placing phones in a communal charging basket or on a labeled shelf; physical cues remove ambiguity and make compliance easy. Frame no-phone zones not as punishments but as shared commitments to the family's emotional health: uninterrupted eye contact at dinner, better sleep when screens are absent from bedrooms, and clearer concentration during homework. Modeling matters more than enforcing; when adults honor the same rules, children internalize them faster and resist less. For teens, negotiate reasonable exceptions—an on-call parent, limited access for late-night study—so the policy feels fair rather than authoritarian.

Monitoring services such as Bark and Covenant Eyes can be powerful allies when employed transparently and sparingly. I personally use these in my own home and have had great success with them. These platforms scan messages, social media, and web activity for red flags—cyberbullying, predatory behavior, self-harm indicators, and explicit content—and can send alerts that give parents a chance to intervene before harm escalates.

But technical surveillance without conversation erodes trust and misses the teaching moment. Be explicit with your child about what is being monitored and why, and calibrate the level of oversight to age and circumstance: younger children may need more protective monitoring, while older teens deserve negotiated agreements that trade some privacy for accountability.

Remember, these services are an entry point for discussion, not a substitute for ongoing education about consent, the permanence of digital footprints, and how to ask for help when something online feels wrong.

Passwords and account protections are the backbone of any device-lock strategy. Strong, unique passphrases and two-factor authentication (2FA) dramatically reduce the risk of unauthorized access, digital impersonation, or accidental account changes that can have real-world consequences.

Teach children the principles early: use long passphrases rather than single words, never reuse passwords across important accounts, and treat login information with the same care as house keys. A family password manager provides a practical compromise—parents can securely store shared credentials and control access levels while tutoring children in responsible management.

For younger kids, maintain master control but involve them gradually; for teens, transition responsibility incrementally while retaining safeguards for purchases, app installations, and changes to privacy settings. Consider the role of biometrics and device passcodes thoughtfully: they are convenient but should be paired with broader account protections and parental oversight when appropriate.

Turning policy into practice requires a methodical setup and a dose of routine maintenance. Start by inventorying every device and account connected to your household network—phones, tablets, game consoles, smart speakers, and streaming devices—and create family or child profiles where supported. Enable device encryption, set automatic software updates, and configure remote-wipe or Find My Device capabilities so a lost phone doesn't become a privacy catastrophe. Use router-level content filters or Domain Name System (DNS)-based solutions to apply consistent limits across devices, including those that don't support platform parental controls. Back up important data so enforcement actions don't become unintended crises.

Finally, plan concrete responses to violations: when an alert or infraction appears, lead with conversation—ask what happened, listen to context, and explain the harm—then apply proportionate consequences that focus on restoration (temporary loss of privileges, supervised digital time, or a learning assignment about online safety).

The human work—education, empathy, and consistent modeling—is as important as the tech. Teach children how to recognize scams, how to pause before sharing intimate images, and how to respond to cyberbullying or predatory behavior. Use real examples (without shaming) to illustrate risks and praise moments of responsible behavior. Schedule regular family tech check-ins—a monthly "digital summit"—to revisit rules, adjust limits, and invite teens to propose experiments for greater independence. This collaborative approach builds buy-in and prepares adolescents for autonomy rather than setting them up for covert rebelliousness.

Locking down devices is ultimately about safeguarding the conditions for growth: sleep, attention, secure identity, and meaningful relationships. When technical controls are paired with transparent communication, negotiated autonomy, and consistent adult modeling, households can create resilient systems that protect young people while teaching them to manage their own digital lives. Make the plan explicit, keep the conversation alive, and remember that the goal is not perfect control but a home where technology supports flourishing rather than undermining it. Begin with one concrete step today—a family meeting, a phone-free dinner, a password audit—and let that action become the first rung in a ladder toward safer, wiser device use.

It is absolutely okay to decide your child doesn't get a device until you feel they are ready. In a culture that treats phones and tablets as inevitable rites of passage, choosing to wait can feel lonely—or even judged—but it is a legitimate, protective parenting choice. Devices are not neutral tools; they are entry points into a complex, adult-designed world of algorithms, strangers, sexualized content, and relentless peer pressure. For many families, especially those healing from trauma or working to build strong communication and boundary skills, delaying device ownership buys essential time: time to grow emotional maturity, to learn social and problem-solving skills in real life, and to develop the habits—sleep hygiene, focus, impulse control—that screens so easily erode. Choosing delay is an intentional act of stewardship, not deprivation.

Many parents hand a device to a child because it buys quiet time—an easy answer to exhaustion or logistical pressure. That's understandable; parenting is hard and screens can be lifelines in the moment. But when devices become the default babysitter, they also become the place where children learn risky behaviors and where predators and peer coercion can take root. It's okay to refuse convenience for long-term safety. If you're feeling the pressure to "fit in" with other families or to keep a child occupied while you juggle work and chores, plan alternatives that give you breathing room without outsourcing development: a basket of new craft materials, audiobooks or podcasts chosen by you, supervised playdates, outdoor free play with neighborhood rules, rotating responsibilities with other caregivers, or short bursts of structured activity (puzzles, simple science kits, creative challenges). These are not perfect substitutes for childcare help, so line up practical supports—trusted neighbors, grandparents, or caregiver cooperatives—so you don't shoulder this alone.

You will face pushback: your child's peers will have devices, teachers may expect digital homework access, and other parents may ask why your child can't join a group chat or hangout. Have a clear, calm script ready and a family policy that you state with confidence: "We don't do personal devices until X (age or milestone). We'll still do group activities, and we'll make sure homework and socializing are possible through supervised channels." Offer solutions when the world around you assumes phone access: volunteer to host in-person study groups, arrange that chores or earning privileges can buy supervised screen time, or provide a parent-controlled device for essential tasks only (homework, scheduled calls) while maintaining no-phone nights. Consistency matters more than perfection—when you stick to a clearly explained policy, children gradually accept it as normal, not punishment.

Finally, prepare a pathway to readiness so the decision to delay is constructive rather than merely prohibitive. Define measurable markers of responsibility—consistent completion of chores and homework, demonstrated good sleep habits, honest reporting of uncomfortable situations, participation in family tech-safety lessons—and tie device privileges to those markers. Teach the skills they'll need before handing over a screen: critical thinking about media, privacy and password basics, refusal scripts for sexting or pressure, and a practice in preserving evidence and asking for help. When you do introduce devices, do it as a coached transition—an apprenticeship in digital citizenship with clear limits, monitoring in place, and a written family agreement. That way you aren't denying childhood pleasures; you're timing access so your child gets the protection, maturity, and parental partnership they need to use technology safely.

CHAPTER NOTES:

Chapter 23

The Intersection of Foster Care, Vulnerability, and Human Trafficking

We have fostered for two decades and welcomed more than 200 children into our home. That experience is not a résumé item so much as a living map of pain, resilience, and system failure. Over and over, we have watched how foster care — intended to protect — can become the very intersection where vulnerability meets exploitation.

Foster care is meant to be shelter; too often, it **UNINTENTIONALLY** becomes a place where young people slip through the cracks and fall into the hands of traffickers because their needs were misunderstood, their behaviors were punished, or their instability was treated as the problem rather than the symptom.

Let me be **VERY** clear, I do not believe that this is intentional by the system itself. In fact, often workers want to do more, but more times than not, policy overrides common sense. Our system, sadly, has become " parent welfare" and we are failing.

This chapter is both a witness and a call to arms. It lays out how vulnerability in the foster-care system creates openings for human trafficking, why children "bounce around" homes, how misdiagnosis and negative labeling make matters worse, and what each of us — as neighbors, professionals, policymakers, mentors, and potential foster parents — can do to close those gaps.

How vulnerability becomes opportunity

Vulnerability is not a personality trait; it is a circumstance created by loss, isolation, and unmet need. For children in foster care, these vulnerabilities are often multiple and cumulative: trauma from abuse or neglect, disrupted attachments, poverty, lack of consistent schooling, and fragmented healthcare. Traffickers are predators who look for seams in a fabric — the places where a community has frayed. They do not need force and chains; they need access to children who are alone, desperate for belonging, or who fall outside the attention of caring adults.

Several dynamics make foster youth particularly susceptible:

- **Placement instability:** Children who move repeatedly between homes, group placements, or shelters lose the protective benefit of stable adult relationships. Each move erodes trust, creates gaps in supervision, and increases exposure to unsafe adults.
- **Runaway behavior:** Young people with unresolved trauma often run from care to escape pain or punishments. Traffickers cultivate friendships and offer a façade of normalcy, housing, money, or affection — all of which can feel like rescue.
- **System invisibility:** Caseworkers are overloaded, records are incomplete, and coordinated services are sparse. A child can be labeled "behavioral" and lose access to therapeutic supports that might reduce risk.
- **Misdiagnosis and labeling:** Trauma symptoms are frequently misread as defiance, conduct disorder, or simply "acting out." When children are medicated or punished instead of treated for trauma, the underlying

needs remain unaddressed, and the child remains vulnerable.

- **Aging out without support:** Youth who leave the foster system without a family are at high risk for homelessness and exploitation. Without employment, housing, or relationships, survival becomes the priority — and traffickers provide shortcuts. Supports are available; there are multiple programs that are fantastic for youth. However, youth often refuse to "willingly remain in the system."

Real stories, composite but true

Consider the story of "Maya," a composite drawn from years of fostering. She arrived at 14, angry, mistrustful, and labeled "difficult." Her trauma showed up as sexualized behavior and defiance. Schools and caretakers focused on discipline; there was little accessible therapy or sustained attachment work. After three placements in two years, she ran away. A man offered a place to stay and a sense of worth. Within weeks, she was trapped in a cycle of exploitation that began with "help" and ended in isolation. Maya's trajectory is not rare — it is the predictable result of missed opportunities.

Or "Evan," who aged out at 18 with no family and minimal job skills. He grew up in the system and was tired of it, so he refused the offered services. He bounced between couch-surfing and temporary work; traffickers recruited him for labor in exploitative conditions, hiding the abuse behind "easy money."

These are not horror stories meant to shock; they are examples of how ordinary failures lead to catastrophic outcomes.

Why "negative behaviors" are warning signs, not character flaws

Behavior that caregivers call "negative" is often a communication: a child saying, without words, that something is wrong. Hypervigilance, anger, hyper sexualization, withdrawal, substance use, truancy — these are distress signals. When systems respond to these behaviors with expulsion, punitive placements, medication without therapy, or multiple moves, they effectively increase the child's exposure to trafficking.

Misdiagnosis compounds harm. A child with reactive attachment, complex PTSD, or developmental trauma will not respond to standard disciplinary approaches. They need consistent, trauma-informed care that rebuilds trust, teaches regulation skills, and repairs relationships. Without this, they remain easy targets.

How traffickers recruit from foster systems

Trafficking is a process, not just a single event. Common tactics include:

- **Befriending and grooming:** Traffickers create the illusion of family, attention, and acceptance. For a teen who's been told they are a burden, a trafficker's interest can be intoxicating.
- **Exploiting need:** Offers of food, housing, clothes, or a job are often the bait. For a youth who has been bounced from home to home, these are powerful draws.
- **Coercion under the guise of care:** Traffickers may parlay caretaking into control, isolating youth from other supports and making escape difficult.

146

- **Online entrapment:** Social media platforms and apps become recruitment sites where youth with disrupted supervision are approached and groomed.

Prevention requires both protection and connection

If we accept that exploitation thrives where need meets isolation, then prevention must shrink the distance between a young person and reliable, sustained care. Prevention is not only a set of services — it is a relational architecture designed to make every child visible and supported.

Key prevention strategies

- **Stability and permanency:** Prioritize fewer placements and targeted interventions that keep children in family-like settings whenever possible. Family-finding, kinship placement, and permanency planning reduce churn.
- **Trauma-informed training for everyone:** Foster parents, teachers, caseworkers, law enforcement, and judges must understand trauma responses. Training should focus on attachment repair, de-escalation, and therapeutic parenting.
- **Early screening for exploitation risk:** Regular risk assessments that include questions about online contact, running behaviors, and sudden changes in peers can flag danger early.
- **Invest in mental health and wraparound supports:** Access to culturally competent therapists, psychiatric care when needed (not as first-line response), school-based supports, and individualized educational plans reduces risk.
- **Specialized placements for high-risk youth:** Therapeutic foster homes and small, well-

supervised programs for children with complex trauma provide consistency and expertise.

- **Mentors and community bonds**: Stable, supported adult mentors reduce isolation. Volunteer mentorship programs, faith communities, athletic programs, and apprenticeships create belonging that traffickers cannot replicate.
- **Transitional housing and life-skills training:** For youth aging out of care, structured housing, job training, and ongoing case management are essential buffers against exploitation.
- **Data and coordination**: Cross-system data sharing (with privacy protections) helps track patterns, identify trafficking hotspots, and ensure continuity of care across placements and schools.

What foster parents, neighbors, and advocates can do today?

- **Learn trauma-informed parenting**: Seek out training, supervision, and peer support. Understand that behaviors are messages, not willful misbehavior.
- **Fight placement churn:** Advocate to caseworkers for stability; document what works; push for wraparound services rather than moves.
- **Build relationships, not just rules**: Time and consistency are protective factors. Shared meals, predictable routines, and steady presence matter.
- **Watch for red flags for trafficking:** unexplained gifts, multiple phones, secretive late-night activity, sudden withdrawal, unexplained money or expensive items, or older "boyfriends" or "girlfriends" who control access.

- **Engage schools:** Advocate for educational stability and supports that reduce school absences and disengagement.
- **Mentor, sponsor, volunteer:** You do not have to be a foster parent to make a difference. Mentors and volunteers provide crucial stability and adult connection.
- **Advocate for policy changes:** funding for mental health, smaller caseloads for caseworkers, specialized training, and resources for transitional youth all reduce trafficking risk.
- **Report concerns:** If you suspect trafficking or imminent harm, report to local law enforcement or your country's human trafficking hotline. Prompt reporting can save lives.

Language matters: dignity over deficit

Too often, the system talks about "bad kids," "problem behavior," or "system failures" in ways that strip young people of dignity. We must change the narrative to one of survivors, children with reactions to trauma, and young people who need and deserve repair, not punishment. Language shapes responses: when we name children as wounded rather than willful, services follow.

A plea for more parents, more patience, more persistence

We need more families willing to do the hard work of parenting children who come with histories. This work requires training, respite, support groups, and financial investment — and it yields returns that ripple outward. Every child who finds a stable home is one less child traffickers can target.

If you are considering fostering, know this: you will spend more time knitting together broken trust than you will disciplining. The majority of moments will be mundane and tender — homework, meals, a prom dress. Some will be agonizing. But the outcomes are life-changing. Your presence could turn a path away from exploitation and toward a life where a young person can learn to hope again.

Systems must change, too

Individuals matter, but we cannot rely only on the goodwill of families. Policies must change to reduce risk: lower caseloads, better training, guaranteed mental health services, and integrated anti-trafficking protocols across child welfare, education, law enforcement, and healthcare. Funding must follow outcomes instead of processes. Data must be used to identify hotspots and tailor interventions before youth fall through the cracks.

A closing charge

The intersection of foster care, vulnerability, and human trafficking is not an inevitable crossroads — it is a set of conditions we create by tolerating instability, ignoring trauma, and underfunding care. We have seen this in hundreds of children: the missed referrals, the misdiagnoses, the homes that could not hold them, the aging-out youth who keep getting "tough love" when what they needed was a family, a mentor, a therapist, a job, and someone who believed they were worth saving.

We are not helpless. Each of us can act — by opening our homes, mentoring a youth, advocating for policy change, supporting trauma-informed services, or simply refusing to let a child's behaviors define their future. Traffickers exploit what our systems allow. If we change the systems — and change our responses — we cut off the opportunity for exploitation.

Friends, if this chapter moves you, let it move you to action. Foster a child, support programs that stabilize placements, advocate for trauma-informed training in your community, or mentor a teenager who needs a steady adult. The work is difficult, but it is the work that saves lives. The children who enter foster care are not statistics; they are futures. With collective will, compassion, and persistent action, we can make those futures anything but inevitable— for every child who needs a refuge, and for the families and communities who can offer one.

CHAPTER NOTES:

Chapter 24

Courtship & Care

Protecting Young People in Dating Situations

Dating is a complicated rite of passage. For many families and communities, it is a time to watch a young person step from childhood into adolescence and independence. But the world that shapes those early experiences has changed dramatically in a few short decades. The ways young people meet, communicate, and express intimacy — especially through screens — create risks that previous generations rarely faced. This chapter is about balancing care and respect for growing autonomy while protecting young people from harm: emotional, physical, and digital. It argues that many children are not developmentally ready for dating as it exists today, explains the particular dangers present now, and offers practical guidance for parents, caregivers, educators, and teens themselves.

Why dating is different now

When we remember "how it used to be," two things stand out: our social worlds were smaller and slower. Peer groups were localized; meeting someone often meant seeing them in person at school, community events, or through family connections. Information traveled more slowly, and the adult world acted as a buffer. Today, social media, instant messaging, and ubiquitous smartphones collapse distance and time. Young people can form intense relationships almost overnight, and those relationships can be amplified, recorded, shared, and weaponized.

This acceleration has three consequences:

- Intensity without time: Relationships can feel very serious before young people have had the chance to develop the emotional regulation and perspective that come with age and experience.
- Visibility and permanence: Private conversations, images, or mistakes can be saved, spread, and used against someone — increasing risk and shame.
- Reduced adult mediation: Online spaces often lack the informal adult oversight that helped moderate behavior in the past, making it harder to spot and interrupt unhealthy dynamics early.

Developmental readiness:

Kids are still growing.

Biologically and psychologically, children and early adolescents are not simply "small adults." Their brains — especially the prefrontal cortex, which governs impulse control, long-term planning, and risk assessment — continue maturing well into the mid-20s. Emotional skills like managing jealousy, recognizing manipulation, and setting healthy boundaries also take practice and guidance. Expecting children to negotiate romantic relationships that require maturity, perspective, and consistent consent is unrealistic and risky.

Common dangers in youth dating

- **Emotional harm and identity confusion**

  Early dating can lead to intense attachments that shape a young person's self-worth and choices. Breakups that might be manageable for older teens can feel catastrophic to younger children, contributing to anxiety, depression, or social withdrawal.

- **Dating violence and coercion**

  Dating violence is not limited to physical assault. It includes emotional abuse, controlling behaviors, manipulation, threats, sexual coercion, and digital harassment. Young people are vulnerable because they may not recognize abusive patterns and may feel shame or fear about telling adults.

- **Sexual pressure and risky sexual behavior**

  Technology and media sexualize young people, and peer pressure can push minors into sexual situations before they are ready to consent or understand the consequences.

- **Digital dangers: sexting, stalking, and image exploitation**

  Images and messages can be shared beyond the intended recipient. Revenge porn, persistent unwanted contact, doxing, and public shaming are all modern risks that can cause long-term harm.

- **Peer pressure and social status**

  Dating can become a status marker, driving risky decisions to fit in or to keep a relationship visible to peers, which can mean tolerating bad treatment.

- **Isolation from support networks**

  Abusive relationships often isolate the young person from friends and family, cutting off the very sources that would help them gain perspective and support.

Recognizing dating violence and abuse

Signs that a young person may be in an unhealthy or abusive relationship include:

- Sudden changes in mood, academic performance, or social life.
- Persistent texting/calls from a partner that interferes with sleep or school.
- Withdrawal from friends, family, or activities they once loved.
- Wearing clothing or altering behavior to appease a partner.
- Frequent injuries or explanations that seem inconsistent.
- Extreme jealousy, monitoring (demanding passwords, tracking location), or public shaming online.
- Fearful statements about displeasing the partner or strong efforts to hide the relationship.

- If you suspect abuse, take the young person seriously, listen without judgment, and prioritize their safety. Validate their feelings and help them access counseling, school support staff, or local youth services.

When we were kids: what was different — and why nostalgia can mislead

Many parents remember their own adolescence as freer in some ways: more unsupervised play, fewer digital records of mistakes, and social circles that moved more slowly. For many, "back in the day, 16 was the magic number" — a commonly accepted age when dating was considered appropriate and allowed. That cultural benchmark helped set expectations and boundaries within families and peer groups. But context matters. Past risks existed (coercion, emotional pain, teen pregnancy), yet the volume and speed of today's risks are different. The permanence of digital content, the scale of public shaming, and the sophistication of online exploitation are new. Comparing across eras should inform empathy but not minimize present dangers or justify inaction.

Practical guidance for parents and caregivers

- **Start early with values and language**

  Talk about respect, consent, boundaries, and media literacy before romantic feelings arise. Use simple, age-appropriate language and reinforce that relationships should add to, not take away from, a person's sense of self.

- **Set clear, consistent boundaries**

  Rules about when dating is appropriate, what form it can take (group vs. one-on-one), and digital expectations are not about control — they are about safety. Involve young people in setting these rules to encourage buy-in.

- **Teach concrete skills**

  Role-play how to say "no," how to ask for consent, and how to leave an uncomfortable situation. Teach them to recognize red flags: intense jealousy, attempts to isolate, making threats, or pressure for sexual activity.

- **Monitor with respect**

  Know who your child is spending time with, both in person and online. Use parental controls appropriately but combine them with open conversation so monitoring isn't the only strategy.

- **Model healthy relationships**

  Young people learn from what they see. Demonstrating respectful conflict resolution, clear boundaries, and mutual support in your relationships teaches more than any lecture.

- **Address digital safety explicitly**

  Talk about sexting risks, how quickly images can be shared, and strategies for refusing pressure to send images. Teach how to block, report, and document abuse online.

- **Maintain connection and open communication**

  Make it easy for your child to tell you about problems without fear of punishment. Reassure them that seeking help will not automatically mean the end of freedom but will prioritize safety.

- **Collaborate with schools and communities**

  Advocate for relationship education in schools that covers consent, digital safety, and emotional regulation. Encourage community programs that provide supervised social opportunities.

Practical guidance for young people (age-appropriate advice)

- Keep dating in group settings until you have good reason to trust someone one-on-one.
- Maintain friendships and activities outside any relationship.
- Trust your instincts. If something feels off, it probably is.
- Know that no one has the right to control you, demand passwords, or make you do things you don't want to do.
- Save evidence and files if you are threatened or harassed online (screenshots, timestamps) and tell a trusted adult.
- There is no shame in ending a relationship or seeking help.
- Safety planning and immediate steps if there's danger

- If you or a young person is in immediate danger: contact emergency services.
- Limit contact with the abusive person and block them online where possible.
- Reach out to trusted adults, counselors, or local youth services. If in school, inform a counselor or administrator about the issue.
- Create a physical safety plan: trusted places to go, people to call, and ways to leave safely.

The role of policy and community

Protecting young people requires systemic support:

Schools should include comprehensive relationship education and clear reporting pathways for abuse.

Community organizations should provide supervised social options for teens and accessible counseling services.

Online platforms must do more to prevent and respond to the exploitation of minors — and families should be aware of reporting tools on each platform.

Legal protections and clarity about consent and age-of-consent laws should be accessible to families without creating fear about seeking help.

The goal is not to cage curiosity or delay maturity indefinitely. It is to recognize that in today's environment, many children lack the emotional and cognitive tools to handle the full weight of modern dating safely. Courtship and early romantic interactions can be healthy when they happen in a context that includes adult guidance, skill-building, and intentional limits. Protecting young people means teaching them how to recognize respect, demand care, and seek help without shame. It means reshaping our nostalgia — even the memory that 16 once felt like the magic number — into practical policies and practices that match the realities of today's world — so that when young people do enter romantic relationships, they do so with knowledge, safety, and dignity.

For parents, educators, and guardians: this is ongoing work. Keep the conversations open, stay informed about new technologies and trends, and remember that your presence — steady, nonjudgmental, and attentive — is one of the best protections a young person can have.

Different Way — Courtship, the Third Person Rule, and Growing Together

It is no surprise that we may do things a bit differently with dating. As previously stated in multiple chapters, we have a high-trauma household. Multiple children are already survivors of sexual abuse, human trafficking, and physical abuse. Regardless of a child's history, this is another way that can be adapted to preserve their childhoods safely.

Some families and communities choose an intentional approach to early romantic life that prioritizes emotional maturity, safety, and friendship over private one-on-one dating. This model—often described as courting—focuses on allowing attraction and closeness to develop within a structured, supervised context so young people can mature together without the pressure and privacy that often accelerate sexualization and risky behavior. At its core are a few clear principles: emphasize courting rather than dating, require a third person to be present when young people are together, discourage physical contact until an agreed level of maturity is reached, and encourage friendship-first development through shared activities that reveal character and values.

The third-person rule means that when two young people who are exploring interests spend time together, they do so with at least one trusted adult or responsible third person present. The presence is intended to be a buffer, not intrusive supervision: it reduces opportunities for pressure or manipulation, keeps interactions public and less likely to escalate into intense private dynamics, and gives adults the chance to notice relational patterns and step in if unhealthy behavior appears. Practically, this looks like group activities, family-hosted gatherings, or a shared adult chaperone joining outings in public settings. Logistics are simple but essential: parents know where teens will be, who is present, and when the activity ends.

Courting instead of dating shifts the emphasis from secretive romance to getting to know someone's character, family, and values through conversation and shared purpose. Activities centered on common interests—volunteering, hobbies, study groups, sports, or community projects— create natural opportunities to learn about each other without making physical intimacy the focal point. Introductions to both families happen early and openly, and relationship progressions are slow, deliberate, and discussed with parental involvement rather than decided behind closed doors.

A no-physical-contact boundary helps prevent early sexualization of relationships while adolescents are still developing impulse control and understanding of consent. This boundary keeps emotional intensity manageable and lowers the chance of decisions that can be amplified by digital sharing. Families should define what "no physical contact" means in clear terms—whether that means no private holding hands, no kissing, no sexual touching, and whether brief public gestures (like a family-welcomed hug) are allowed. In our home, we allow side hugs only with two people who are "courting." Some families tie changes in the rules to age or demonstrated maturity, and it's helpful to teach alternatives for expressing affection, such as verbal affirmation, acts of service, and shared time.

Teaching concrete skills is central to making this model work. Young people need scripts for consent and refusal, practice setting boundaries, and conflict-resolution skills. Role-play helps them learn to say, "I'm not comfortable with that," and to leave a situation that feels unsafe. Parents and caregivers should model healthy communication and provide spaces to debrief mistakes without shaming curiosity. When rules are broken, restorative measures—mediated conversations, reduced privileges, or supervised activities—help repair trust more effectively than purely punitive responses.

Addressing pushback requires empathy and involvement, while still having those non-negotiables. Teens may see the rules as restrictive or out of step with peers; explaining the safety rationale, involving them in shaping guidelines, and reinforcing that different families make different choices can reduce alienation. Monitoring should be done with respect: clear family agreements set expectations, and keeping lines of communication open makes it more likely that teens will seek help if something goes wrong. Families should celebrate positive choices and honest communication, so teens feel respected rather than policed.

This approach reduces risks of dating violence, coercion, and early sexual activity while helping young people develop social skills and emotional resilience in the context of friendships. It lowers opportunities for compromising digital media, strengthens family and community ties through shared responsibility, and allows teens to make informed, timely choices about romantic progression. Exceptions can be considered deliberately as teens demonstrate sustained responsibility and healthy communication, but any relaxation of rules should involve both families and be documented in conversation. If a young person reports pressure, coercion, or abuse, private interactions should cease immediately, and adults should seek support from school counselors, therapists, or legal authorities when necessary.

Ultimately, the goal is not to deny normal feelings but to structure early relationships so that attraction matures into a respectful partnership rather than becoming primarily a sexual presence. When implemented with clarity, empathy, and participation from teens, the third-person rule, courting practices, and clear boundaries give young people space to grow together as friends first—building character, communication, and mutual respect—so that if and when they choose greater intimacy, they do so from a place of readiness and safety.

We talk more about this in Chapter 26.

CHAPTER NOTES:

Chapter 25

Caring for the Caregivers

How Non-Offending Parents and Families Survive, Protect, and Heal

One chapter that is often missing from books like this — and that I believe must be included now — is a detailed, compassionate guide for non-offending caregivers: the parents, guardians, grandparents, foster and adoptive parents, and other family members who must survive the disclosure and then hold the child through what follows. I know that in previous chapters, some of these things are listed, but I wanted parents to have the ability to refer to a chapter quickly.

In my work and in my life, I've seen how much damage happens not only from the abuse itself but from what comes after: overwhelmed caregivers who shut down, families that fracture, children who are left to grieve alone while the adults "handle it," and an absence of practical, step-by-step guidance that centers both safety and caregiver wellbeing.

You bear two impossible jobs at once after a disclosure: you must protect and steer the practical response (safety, reporting, evidence preservation, legal steps) while also being the emotional anchor for a child whose sense of safety has been shattered. That double duty is the most dangerous place to be when you are grieving, furious, or numb. You can't pour from an empty cup — and yet the system often expects you to. This chapter fills that gap. It's for the caregiver who needs concrete scripts, clear priorities, and ways to protect others.

The invisible harm caregivers carry

When a child tells you they were harmed, the world tilts. I cannot overstate how normal your feelings are: shock, rage, guilt, shame, disbelief, the frantic need to "fix" things immediately. In the fog of that first hour, many caregivers do one of three things: they freeze and do nothing, they explode and pursue immediate confrontation, or they try to handle everything themselves without calling for help. Each reaction can unintentionally harm the child or derail an investigation.

I want you to know three truths before we go any further:

- Telling you may be the most courageous step a child ever takes. Believe them.
- You do not need to be stoic or perfect. You need to be steady enough to do the next right thing, and you can ask for help to be steady.
- Your own well-being directly affects your child's recovery. This is not optional self-indulgence — it is a safety issue.

This chapter gives you the roadmap to act in those first hours and days, to protect siblings, to navigate investigations, to find advocacy and therapy, and to do the slower, harder work of family repair. It is practical, faith-rooted when that matters to you, and unapologetically clear about priorities.

Part 1 — The first 24–72 hours: clear priorities and exact words to use.

Immediate priorities — what matters most (in order):

- Safety: move the child to a safe location where the suspected abuser cannot access them. If immediate danger exists, call 911.
- Believe and respond with calm belief and protect the child from further questioning or interrogation.
- Preserve evidence: avoid bathing the child, changing bedding, laundering clothing, or asking the child to reenact the abuse. Preserve devices, messages, clothes, and photographs.
- Report: contact child protective services and/or law enforcement or follow your mandated-reporting obligations. If you're unsure, call a local child advocacy center or one of the national hotlines and ask for guidance.
- Seek medical care if appropriate: a SANE or pediatric forensic exam may be necessary; medical care also addresses immediate injuries, STI prophylaxis, and emotional safety.
- Get advocacy: contact a victim advocate or child advocacy center to help you navigate reporting, medical logistics, and emotional support.

Exact words that protect and stabilize:

You will probably want to ask thousands of questions. Don't. Children often retract or become confused with repeated, leading questioning. Use short, validating, nonleading lines:

- Thank you for telling me. I believe you.

- You did nothing wrong.
- I'm going to keep you safe. I'm going to call people who help children.
- I don't need all the details to help you. If you want to tell me more, you can. If not, that's okay.
- I'm not going to be mad at you.

What not to say or do

- Do not ask for a graphic retelling. Don't press for "exactly what happened" or demand that the child show you what was done.
- Do not express disbelief or immediate blame toward the child or the accused.
- Do not confront the suspected abuser alone. That can endanger the child and destroy evidence.
- Do not make promises you can't keep (e.g., "I'll never tell anyone"). You should be honest about reporting obligations.

Practical checklist for the first hours

- Get the child to a safe place and keep them with a trusted adult who will listen calmly.
- If there is imminent danger, call 911.
- Preserve clothing, bedding, phones, and devices. Note: don't examine photos or messages unless an authority instructs you — take screenshots and preserve originals.
- Write contemporaneous notes: times, exact words the child used, who was present, and your immediate actions. Keep these safe and private.
- Contact your local child advocacy center or hotline for next steps and to arrange medical/forensic care if indicated.

- If you are a mandated reporter, make the report immediately per your laws and workplace policies.

Part 2 — Managing the caregiver's own crisis reaction

Why caregiver self-care is not optional:

When caregivers collapse into grief, anger, or avoidance, children are often left to cope alone or to bear the burden of "protecting" the adults. I have seen entire sibling sets retraumatized because the non-offending parent vanished into a cycle of self-punishment or anger. Your stability is a therapeutic intervention. It will not heal everything, but it will prevent more damage.

Practical steps for emotional regulation in the first days

- Pause and breathe slowly for one minute before taking any call or making any decision. That centering is tiny but powerful.
- Create a short script to use with family and friends so you don't repeat details: "We are addressing a serious safety issue. We will share more when appropriate." Use that to guard the child's privacy.
- Delegate urgent logistics: ask a trusted friend or family member to handle meals, childcare for siblings, or communications. You don't need to be the project manager for every step.
- Seek an advocate now: an advocate can hold your hand through reporting, court processes, and medical visits. They also provide emotional triage and practical steps.

Recognize complicated grief and guilt

Many caregivers feel responsible — "I should have known," "I missed the signs," or "I failed them." Those feelings are normal but—left unchecked—can paralyze action. Guilt is an impulse to repair; convert it to observable acts: document, report, secure medical care, and seek therapy for everyone affected. If you are grieving for a lost sense of safety or for the life you expected, name it. Find spiritual and therapeutic resources to process this sorrow so it doesn't consume your caregiving.

When caregivers are accused or implicated

Sometimes the dynamics are messy: the caregiver may be accused of complicity, or an abusive partner may manipulate reporting. If you face hostility, seek immediate legal advice, a safe advocate, and clear documentation of your actions and observations. Protect your access to the child where you can, document everything, and follow advice from your advocate and legal counsel.

Part 3 — Protecting siblings and other children in the home

Children who witness disruption carry trauma too.

Siblings are not collateral; they need attention even if they weren't directly harmed. Your reactions set the family tone. Avoid pressuring them to "be brave" or to keep secrets. Instead, offer routines, small responsibilities, and age-appropriate explanation.

Practical steps for sibling safety and care

- Immediate separation from the alleged abuser: do not leave siblings alone with the suspected person.
- Maintain routines: consistent mealtimes, bedtimes, and school attendance after a disclosure provide a stabilizing framework.
- Age-appropriate explanation: tell siblings nothing more than they need to know, in plain language. For young children: "Someone did something that was not allowed, and we are keeping everyone safe." For older children: be truthful that an investigation is happening and that adults are working to make the family safe.
- Watch for behavior changes: regression, acting out, withdrawal, somatic complaints. Refer to school counselors and pediatricians if symptoms persist.
- Assign a trusted adult: ensure each child has at least one safe adult to turn to who is not the primary stressed caregiver.

Boundaries in the household to prevent further harm.

- No one-on-one closed-door time with the accused until safety decisions are made.
- Supervised visits only, if any; follow professional safety recommendations.
- Consider temporary protective separation while investigations and safety planning occur.

Part 4 — Navigating reporting, investigations, and legal processes (without losing the child).

Reporting is a protection step, not an accusation of guilt.

Reporting triggers an investigation and protective responses. It does not assume guilt — it starts professional fact-finding. Expect the process to feel invasive and slow. That frustration is normal, but remember the system's purpose is to prioritize the safety and rights of the child.

How to work with child protective services and law enforcement.

- Be factual and calm in your report. Provide dates, observable behaviors, exact quotes from the child, and any physical evidence.
- Ask for the investigator's name, contact info, and expected next steps. Document the call.
- Cooperate with forensic interview schedules — trained interviewers reduce re-traumatization by asking the child questions once in a neutral, supportive environment.
- Expect multiple agency involvement: CPS, law enforcement, local advocacy centers, and possibly prosecution. Maintain a point person (advocate) to coordinate communication.

Protecting the child's wellbeing during investigations.

- Limit repeated retelling: repeated questioning harms; let trained forensic interviewers do the investigative interviewing.
- Continue routines and therapy referrals as needed.
- Keep the child's privacy: avoid social media posts, discussions in public, and exposing them to courtroom or media attention.
- Ask for a victim-centered forensic plan: forensic interviews, SANE exams, and mental-health triage at a child advocacy center are best practice.

When criminal charges are filed.

- Expect an extended timeline. Court processes can take months or years and are emotionally exhausting.
- Consider a victim advocate who can guide you through court appearances, protection orders, and testimony decisions.
- Prepare the child: use developmentally appropriate preparation for court involvement, and request trauma-informed professionals to help.

Part 5 — Finding and coordinating therapeutic care.

Therapy is not optional for many children and families. Most children and families benefit from trauma-informed care. Early intervention prevents chronic symptoms. The right therapist is one who understands child development, trauma, and family systems — ideally someone experienced with forensic survivors.

How to choose clinicians and programs.

- Ask for therapists trained in TF-CBT, play therapy for young children, family therapy, or EMDR for older youth — therapists with trauma specialization are ideal.
- Use child advocacy centers for coordinated referrals; they often have lists of vetted therapists and can help with funding or sliding scale options.
- Consider caregiver therapy too: non-offending parents need processing space to avoid projecting fear or anger onto the child. Family therapy can help rebuild trust and set boundaries.

Coordinating care and services.

- Create a centralized folder (digital or paper) for medical records, therapy notes, CPS and law enforcement reports, court dates, and advocacy contacts.
- Ask therapists for a short plan—goals, frequency, expected milestones—and share it with your advocate when appropriate.
- Keep the child's school informed (with consent) so they can provide accommodations.

Financial barriers and practical solutions.

Therapy costs can be a barrier. Ask about:

- Victim-assistance funds available through local agencies or crime victim compensation.
- Sliding scale clinics, university training clinics, and community mental-health centers.
- Nonprofits and local grants. Advocates can often help apply for emergency funds.

Part 6 — Rebuilding family safety and relationships over the long term.

Safety is the baseline; trust is rebuilt slowly.

Safety plans, transparent routines, and consistent adult behavior are the stitches that help families heal. Rebuilding trust looks different in every household, but it always depends on predictability and accountability.

Concrete family practices that rebuild safety

- **Visible calendars:** publicly posted schedules and who is responsible for caregiver transitions reduce secrecy and anxiety.
- **Two-adult rule:** whenever possible, require two vetted adults to be present with children for activities and mentorship.
- **Supervised interactions:** structured and supervised contact or no contact with the accused, according to professional recommendations.
- **Clear, consistent boundaries:** enforce rules for privacy, technology, and one-on-one time.
- **Regular family check-ins:** brief, scheduled conversations that allow each child to speak about their feelings without pressure.
- **Use simple starters:** "What's one thing that worried you this week?" "What made you feel safe?"

Repair and reconciliation: a careful, professional process

Reconciliation with an abuser, if ever considered, must follow sustained, verified accountability and professional guidance. An apology alone is not restoration. True accountability includes:

- Transparent investigation and legal consequences where indicated.
- Documented behavior change over months or years, verified by professionals.
- Professional therapy for the abuser, with external oversight.
- Safety plans and enforceable boundaries before any contact is considered.

- Most experts recommend separation and robust boundaries rather than early reconciliation; prioritize survivor safety and agency at every step.

Part 7 — Faith, community supports, and navigating congregational responses.

Faith communities can be a source of sanctuary — or harm.

Churches and faith groups can offer food, prayer, advocacy, shelter, and mentorship — but they can also respond poorly if reputation is prioritized over safety. Be prepared to advocate for transparent, victim-centered responses.

How to engage your faith community.

- Request written safeguarding policies and insist on external reporting to civil authorities.
- Ask your pastoral leaders to connect you with trauma-informed counselors and to avoid private, **unmonitored meetings.**
- **Invite your church to support practically:** meals, childcare, transportation, assembling Love Bags, or fundraising for therapy. Practical help reduces caregiver stress and offers dignity.

When your congregation fails you.

If a church minimizes, silences, or pressures you, prioritize safety. Advocate for external oversight, involve an outside advocacy organization, and consider transferring fellowship to a place that honors survivor care and mandatory reporting.

Part 8 — Practical tools: scripts, templates, and checklists you can use now.

Short scripts to tell family and friends:

- **To extended family**: "We're addressing a safety issue involving [child]. Out of respect for their privacy and for the investigation, we will share details when appropriate. Right now, we need practical support: meals, childcare, and prayer."
- **To employers**: "I have an urgent family safety matter and will need to take time to manage medical and legal appointments. I can provide dates and documentation as needed."
- **To the child's school**: "My child is safe at home, and we are coordinating care with local advocates. We request short-term accommodations for homework and check-ins with the counselor."

Checklist for the caregiver's first week.

- Secure immediate physical safety.
- Preserve potential evidence.
- Make the mandated report/contact advocate.
- Arrange medical evaluation if indicated.
- Notify school and relevant caregivers quietly and succinctly.
- Schedule therapy evaluations for the child and caregiver.
- Delegate meals, childcare, and logistics to a trusted network.
- Keep a private binder with notes and documentation.
- Avoid social media sharing or public commentary.
- Sleep when you can. Eat. Breathe.

Template for family safety plan (starter).

- Who is restricted from contact?
- Who can pick up the child from school? (List names and phone numbers).
- Where is the child's safe place if they feel unsafe?
- What is our family code word for emergency pickup?
- How will school and extracurriculars be supervised?
- Who is the advocacy contact (name, phone)?
- Where are key documents stored (binder location, digital backup)?

Part 9 — Lessons from those who have walked this path.

A few brief truths survivors and advocates tell me again and again:

- "Believe me and protect me first. Everything else can wait."
- "Don't make me repeat my story to ten people." (Let trained interviewers do that).
- "Tell me what will happen next. Not 'we'll figure it out' — tell me the steps."
- "Keep my routines."
- Care for my siblings. They are scared too."
- "Don't make the church or family protect the abuser. Protect me."

Part 10 — Long view: the caregiver's covenant to keep going.

This is the hard work of love: showing up morning after morning when the wounds are small and when the anniversaries cut deep. It's choosing predictable meals, attending therapy, enforcing technology limits, teaching language for bodies and consent, and celebrating tiny, real victories: one more night of sleep, a week without bedwetting, the child who goes back to school.

A caregiver's covenant — a short promise you can read aloud.

"I will be present. I will believe. I will hold steady. I will get help when I am overwhelmed. I will protect all my children and ask for support when I cannot. I will not trade my child's safety for shame, reputation, or comfort. I will choose the next right thing — even when it is hard."

Permit yourself to be imperfect and to seek help.

If you are reading this in the middle of the night worrying that you missed something, hear me plainly: missing a sign does not make you a bad parent. It makes you human. What matters now is what you do — the steps you take to keep the child safe, to find professional help, and to protect siblings. Take one call, write one note, put the binder in one place. Call an advocate. Breathe. You do not have to carry this alone.

CHAPTER NOTES:

Chapter 26

How We Do It

" Are they all yours?" "I would hate to see their grocery bill." "How many gallons of milk do you go through a month?" "Did you see all those kids?" People ask like they're trying to solve a riddle. Yes—every one of them is ours. Yes—our grocery bill is larger than our mortgage. Fifty-four gallons of milk a month, and yes, I see them all the time.

My husband and I have opened our home for decades. More than two hundred children have slept under our roof, we've adopted eleven from foster care, and we've watched our biological children grow into adulthood. We're a large, disciplined, intentionally different household. This life was not an accident; it is a choice made because children who come from trauma need homes that are deliberate, steady, and saturated with faith. We shelter survivors of human trafficking. We live with high trauma. We anchor everything in a devout Christian faith. Our family motto— *"When you help a child it helps, but when you lead a child to Christ it heals"*—is not a poster on a wall; it is the lens through which we feed, teach, comfort, and correct.

Raising children today is harder than most people realize. Culture moves faster than we can process and streams competing messages that shape identity before a child has the tools to think critically. That reality demands clarity, courage, and relentless intentionality.

This chapter is not a blueprint for every household. It is our story and our hard-won practice. Some choices will feel extreme; they are. For children carrying deep wounds, extreme care is often the difference between surviving and being healed.

Household Purpose

Our home is intentionally strict because clarity and consistency create safety, respect, and calm. Clear rules reduce daily chaos, minimize conflict, and make expectations obvious to every family member so everyone knows what to expect and why.

Boundaries

We protect personal space through firm boundaries: boys do not enter girls' rooms and girls do not enter boys' rooms. We also do not share couch cushions or blankets. These limits prevent confusion and recurring disputes and help maintain respect for each person's belongings and privacy.

Third-Person Rule

Even between siblings, we follow the third-person rule: interactions, dating, and disputes are handled through the household system or with a neutral third person present rather than in spontaneous one-on-one confrontations. This approach reduces emotional escalation, deters power struggles, and provides a predictable, impartial way to manage relationships and conflicts.

Checks and Balances

The household operates on checks and balances, so responsibility and accountability are evenly distributed. Nothing is left vague or open to interpretation; roles and expectations are documented and observable, which helps prevent favoritism and keeps standards consistent. Each child has the ability to call a family meeting when situations arise.

Jurisdictions (Chores)

Chores are called "Jurisdictions." Assignments rotate on a weekly schedule that updates every week. Each child is responsible for one room for the entire week. This single-room ownership for a week eliminates daily disputes about who did what, fosters pride and responsibility, and simplifies enforcement. This also saves fights in the home for who's responsibility the room is. We get a lot less "I don't know" or "I didn't do it".

Laundry Routine

Laundry follows a predictable rhythm: each room of the house is assigned one specific day per week for laundry. I wash and dry the items; the children are responsible for folding their own clothes and putting them away. This division teaches practical life skills while keeping the household running smoothly.

Dating Policy

We operate dating differently. In our home we believe that we are raising "Husbands and Fathers" and "Wives and Mothers". Dating is permitted beginning at 16, but only with a third person present and always monitored closely by parents. This policy aligns with the third-person rule and ensures safety, transparency, and appropriate boundaries while allowing supervised social development.

Screen Time (Television and Gaming)

Television and gaming are privileges that must be earned—they are not given automatically. Access to screens is contingent on meeting expectations, completing jurisdictions, and maintaining household responsibilities. We set clear media limits—what is allowed, when, and why—and enforce them consistently. Games and consoles are kept in common areas of the home so adults can supervise play.

Earphones are not allowed for children so we can hear conversations and detect any contact with others. We monitor games closely: younger children are not permitted to play gun or gory games; preferred titles are family-friendly options like Just Dance, Mario, and track-and-field style games that encourage activity and cooperative play. This approach reduces exposure to harmful content and helps maintain safety and connection.

Devices and Monitoring

We have a GABB Wireless phone in the home for connecting with friends; each child does not get an individual phone. Once a child begins driving, they receive a regular smartphone. GABB phones are designed for kids with limited functionality—emphasizing calling and texting while restricting app stores, social media, and many typical smartphone distractions—so kids can communicate safely without full smartphone access.

For broader oversight, we use Bark and Covenant Eyes on all devices and platforms that connect to the internet. Bark scans texts, emails, and many social platforms for signs of cyberbullying, sexual content, self-harm, and other concerns and alerts parents when it detects risks. Covenant Eyes focuses on blocking explicit content, providing accountability reports, and helping detect grooming behaviors, including attempts to solicit or exchange explicit photos.

These tools are installed across home devices to ensure consistent monitoring and protection. Even with these precautions, some things have slipped through our radar; incidents have occurred, but they are far less frequent and less severe than they once were. I attribute those incidents to parental error and moments of becoming too comfortable—not to any inherent failure of the monitoring tools themselves. We remain vigilant and regularly review our systems to close gaps and improve oversight.

Belief in Schooling

We do not believe one schooling model fits every child—especially in a large, high-need household. What works for one may fail another. For some of our children, public school has been the right fit; for others, it has not. Their paths have included homeschooling, private Christian schooling, and hybrid programs, each chosen with their specific needs in mind.

Homeschooling has offered flexibility around therapy, court dates, and medical care. It removes daily social pressures that can retraumatize and allows us to match academic pace with emotional readiness. Private Christian schools have provided structure, faith integration, and smaller class sizes where certain children could thrive. Hybrid programs and co-ops have given us the balance of academic rigor and peer interaction while still preserving the therapeutic routines that matter at home.

If you are reconsidering school for your child, begin not with reputation but with **needs**: trauma history, therapy cadence, learning gaps, and social triggers. Use co-ops, tutors, and specialists to fill in where you cannot. Build a weekly rhythm that makes space for quiet, scripture, therapy, play, and focused study. And reassess regularly—quarterly if possible. If a setting isn't helping your child heal and grow, don't be afraid to change it.

Public Outings: Bigs and Littles / Buddy System

When we're in public, we don't move in chaos—we move with systems that keep everyone safe and connected. One of the most important is our **Bigs and Littles buddy system**. Each child is paired with care: an older sibling may sit with a younger one at church, a peer may walk beside a younger child to the car, or two Littles may be partnered with an adult chaperone.

The goal isn't to give older kids authority—adults are always in charge of supervision and decisions. Instead, the system helps children feel secure, reduces anxiety in crowded places, and makes sure no one feels alone. Pairings are intentional and always watched over by adults, so safety and connection stay at the center.

We also have a **special family code word** that everyone knows. If we say that word, the children know exactly what to do. The oldest child calmly guides the younger ones to a safe spot we've already planned, while the adult's step in to handle whatever's happening. Because we've practiced it, the children can move quickly and without fear, confident that they are protected.

And as an adoptive family, we carry one more layer of awareness: each of our children has biological parents out there. Some are wonderful, and we remain in healthy communication with them. Others are not safe and could pose a real danger if contact were attempted in public. This is why our systems matter so much. They don't just keep us organized—they safeguard the hearts and well-being of every child, making sure that love, safety, and belonging are always stronger than fear.

These systems—Bigs and Littles, buddy-ups, our family code word, and our awareness of each child's unique story—help us move as one, giving every child the gift of safety, belonging, and peace of mind in public spaces.

Discipline: Training Toward Freedom

Our home is strict, but it is also a home where structure brings life. We thrive on reality and order, because children flourish when boundaries are clear. For us, discipline is not about shaming; it is about **training toward freedom**.

Structure and boundaries are like safety ropes: they keep children from stumbling into chaos over and over. Discipline without explanation is merely punishment; discipline with love is a formative experience. That is why we speak our values aloud—honesty, respect, responsibility— and explain why they matter in everyday life.

Our routines are non-negotiable: meals, schoolwork, chores, and bedtime. Predictability creates safety. Consequences are never designed to humiliate but to teach repair—through apologies, restitution, or meaningful work that restores what was broken. Responsibilities are given according to age and ability, with adults always holding authority, guidance, and oversight. It took us a long time to get to this, the big transition to this in our home in the last year.

We strive to model the very things we ask of our children: calmness under pressure, confession when we are wrong, and active forgiveness when hurt. In this way, they learn that character is not just taught—it is lived.

We also practice the **Love and Logic** parenting model, which emphasizes empathy, limited choices, and natural or logical consequences. This approach allows children to learn responsibility while still feeling supported.

Do we fail sometimes? Of course. But discipline in our home is not about perfection. It is about growth— becoming better today than we were yesterday, together as a family.

Faith at Home

Faith at home cannot be passive; it must be ritualized and reasoned stories and practices that root a child and train discernment so they can recognize what aligns with our beliefs and what does not. Faith in our house is taught, chosen, and rehearsed. It is sermons at the table and mercy in action. If faith will last after children leave our home, it must be more than a Sunday routine; it must be the scaffolding of daily life. Be deliberate: name your values aloud, practice them visibly, and choose what enters your home—media, friendships, conversations—carefully. If you leave that space empty, someone else will fill it. Sadly, the person willing to fill it may not be a person you want.

Purpose and Benefits

These rules and systems are strict by design—not punitive, but intentional. Clear boundaries, rotating jurisdictions, a predictable laundry schedule, a supervised dating policy, careful device management, thoughtful schooling choices, organized public-outing systems, formative discipline, daily rituals, and deliberate faith formation create fairness, teach responsibility, protect personal space, and reduce household friction. Together they help children internalize accountability and contribute to a calmer, more respectful, and safer home.

CHAPTER NOTES:

Chapter 27

Millstone Ministry

*"If anyone causes one of these little ones—
those who believe in me—to stumble, it would
be better for them to have a large millstone
hung around their neck and to be drowned in
the depths of the sea."*

−Matthew 18:6

I have been working in human trafficking for over a decade, whether in foster care, child advocacy or within law enforcement, but in 2021, Jessica had a real-life situation that took place outside of her home. She contacted me for clarification to get confirmation of what she was seeing. That delivered a truth that broke her heart: people in our own community—men, women, and children—were being bought and sold. That moment changed everything for Jessica. Amy joined our Ministry team in 2022, after losing her daughter Matison to Human Trafficking. With Amy and Jessica at my side, what began as a small, grieving response grew into Millstone Ministry: a Christ-centered calling to educate, advocate, and walk with survivors from rescue to restoration.

Our faith shapes everything we do. We believe the Bible is God's authoritative Word and that every person bears God's image. Out of that conviction, we serve with compassion, humility, and urgency. This is not a job for us; it is a ministry.

What we offer:

We provide free seminars and community training (standard length: 3–4 hours with an intermission). We bring practical prevention tools, survivor-informed education, and clear guidance for responding when trafficking is suspected. All materials and, when applicable, continuing education certificates are provided at no charge. Where logistics require, we may ask for help with modest costs.

Seminar topics (modular and customizable)

- Keeping children safe: practical steps for parents and caregivers.
- Why youth are increasingly at risk and how grooming works.
- Pathways of entry and forms of trafficking (sex, labor, and overlapping abuses).
- Red flags and how to respond safely and legally.
- Understanding the predator's mindset without sensationalizing trauma.
- Survivor testimonies used sensitively to educate and inspire.
- The Dangers of Social Media.
- Faith-Informed discussion of the occult with educational context at special request only.

A trauma-aware approach

We do not sensationalize. Testimonies are shared only with informed consent and supports in place. We warn attendees about potentially triggering content and provide space to step out. Our priority is dignity, safety, and long-term well-being.

Prevention and advocacy

Prevention is central. We equip parents, youth workers, and teens with tools for honest, age-appropriate conversations and digital literacy so young people can protect themselves online and in relationships.

When rescue occurs, advocacy follows

- Transportation and relocation.
- Referrals for substance use and mental health care.
- Victim rights advocacy and court support.
- Mentorship and job networking.
- Practical aid for immediate needs.

Matison's Love Bags — street outreach

Born of grief, led by Amy:

Amy lost her daughter, Matison, to trafficking. Out of her grief, she created the Matison's Love Bags Street outreach team so that Matison's name would become a bridge to help rather than only a story of sorrow. Amy leads the team with quiet courage; each Love Bag is prepared with prayer and care.

What Matison's Love Bags provides

- Street outreach by trained, trauma-informed volunteers who build rapport, offer resources, and make safe referrals.
- Dignity-preserving Love Bags (male and female). containing hygiene items, socks, bottled water, nonperishable snacks, and a discreet

resource. card with hotline numbers and ways to contact Millstone Ministry.

How you can help Matison's Love Bags

- Donate travel-size hygiene items, socks, new underwear, bottled water, nonperishable snacks, small first-aid items, zipper/toiletry bags (NEW only).
- Give $10–$20 gift cards (fast-food, Walmart/Meijer, gas) for immediate needs.
- Volunteer for supervised outreach shifts (trauma-informed training and background checks required).
- Host an assembly night to pack Love Bags—include a prayer card and an encouraging note in each bag.
- Pray for the outreach team, for survivors, and for the protection and wisdom of outreach teams.

Safety and partnership

All outreach and advocacy are conducted with volunteer safety and survivor well-being in mind. We coordinate with local law enforcement and social services and train volunteers in boundaries, trauma-informed engagement, and crisis response. Our goal is always to offer options, resources, and a safe point of contact—never coercion.

Practical needs

Immediate needs that make a real difference:

- Small gift cards ($10–$20) for food, clothing, and gas (fast-food, Walmart/Meijer, gas) carried by volunteers and, when appropriate, used to meet urgent needs without compromising safety.

- Monetary donations to sustain outreach and expand services.
- Volunteers, prayer, and partnership from churches and community groups.

Millstone Ministry is a 501(c)(3) nonprofit. Donations are tax-deductible as allowed by law. Your gift helps rescue and restore survivors.

How to partner with us

- Host a seminar: provide a venue, a light intermission snack, and invite the community.
- Support outreach: donate items or gift cards, assemble Love Bags, or join a supervised outreach shift.
- Advocate: mentor a survivor, volunteer for court support, help with job networking, or connect us with local agencies.
- Pray, we simply cannot do what we do without it, pray for guidance, safety, and for us to continue to bring the darkness to light.

From the heart

Human trafficking thrives in the shadows, and the light that chases it back is made of ordinary people willing to act. If you belong to a church, a school, a neighborhood group, or simply a family that wants to do better, join us: host a seminar so your community can learn to spot grooming and respond safely; help assemble or donate Matison's Love Bags for street outreach; give a few small gift cards that meet urgent needs without compromising safety; volunteer your time for court support, mentorship, or job-skills work; and above all, pray for survivors, for those still trapped, and for the rescue teams who stand in the breach. Every small, steady act—an hour, a box of supplies, a listening presence—becomes a bridge out of exploitation.

Our ministry is both practical and pastoral. From rescue to restoration, we support and watch victims become survivors. We bring trauma-aware training, advocacy, and tangible aid, and we also bring presence: quiet listening, prayer when words fail, and the consistent, patient care that helps survivors rebuild trust one day at a time.

This work asks for two hard gifts from communities—courage to look unflinchingly at an ugly reality and compassion to respond without judgment. You don't have to fix everything; take one faithful step and let it lead to the next.

If you are ready to stand with us, email us at info@millstoneministrymi.com or send donations or supplies to P.O. Box 544, Owosso, MI 48867.

Millstone Ministry is a 501(c)(3); gifts are tax-deductible as allowed by law.

Amy, Jessica, and I walk this road together—strategizing, advocating, and sitting in the small, sacred moments where healing begins. Join us in turning grief into action, secrecy into testimony, and brokenness into restoration.

— **Angela (Founder), with Amy and Jessica**

From Left to Right
Amy Robinson, Angela Rodgers-Dudley, Jessica Dietzel

Appendix A

National & Local Hotlines and Reporting Resources

If a child is in immediate danger, call 911 (or your country's emergency number) now. Do not delay consulting this book.

Quick reference — national U.S. hotlines and services

- Emergency: 911 — immediate danger, medical emergency, or violent crisis.
- National Suicide & Crisis Lifeline: 988 — 24/7 crisis counseling for suicidal ideation or emotional crisis.
- National Human Trafficking Hotline: 1-888-373-7888 • Text: 233733 (BEFREE) • humantraffickinghotline.org — report trafficking, get help, locate survivor services.
- National Center for Missing & Exploited Children (NCMEC) / CyberTipline: 1-800-THE-LOST (1-800-843-5678) • missingkids.org/cybertipline — report online sexual exploitation, child pornography, or missing children.
- Childhelp National Child Abuse Hotline: 1-800-4-A-CHILD (1-800-422-4453) • childhelphotline.org — 24/7 crisis intervention, information, and referrals for suspected child abuse.
- RAINN (Rape, Abuse & Incest National Network) / National Sexual Assault Hotline:

1-800-656-HOPE (1-800-656-4673) • rainn.org — crisis support, local rape-crisis center referrals, online chat.
- National Domestic Violence Hotline: 1-800-799-SAFE (1-800-799-7233) • Text: START to 88788 • thehotline.org — shelter, safety planning, legal and advocacy referrals.
- National Runaway Safeline: 1-800-RUNAWAY (1-800-786-2929) • 1800runaway.org — help and resources for runaway or at-risk youth.
- SAMHSA National Helpline (substance use & mental health treatment): 1-800-662-HELP (1-800-662-4357) • samhsa.gov — treatment referrals and support.
- The Trevor Project (LGBTQ+ youth): 1-866-488-7386 • Text/CHAT: 678678 • thetrevorproject.org — 24/7 crisis intervention and resources for LGBTQ+ young people.
- FBI — Internet Crime/Online Exploitation: Report to IC3 at ic3.gov and contact your local FBI field office for online extortion, sextortion, or cross-jurisdictional crimes.

How to find local numbers and services

Local Child Protective Services / Department of Children and Families: search "[your county/state] child protective services" or visit your state government website. If you cannot find it quickly, call your local police non-emergency line and ask for the child-protective services phone number.

Local law enforcement non-emergency number — call to report concerns that are not immediate emergencies; they can advise on next steps and referrals.

Local SANE / sexual-assault forensic exam locations and child advocacy centers: check your county health department, hospital emergency department, or National

Children's Alliance (nationalchildrenalliance.org) for nearby child-friendly forensic exam centers.

Local victim-services and domestic-violence shelters: often listed on the National Domestic Violence Hotline website and through 211 services.

Poison control (if relevant): 1-800-222-1222 (U.S.) — for accidental ingestions or suspected poisoning.

Online reporting & resources

- NCMEC CyberTipline (report online sexual exploitation): missingkids.org/cybertipline
- National Human Trafficking Hotline (online reporting and live chat): humantraffickinghotline.org/report
- IC3 (Internet Crime Complaint Center) for online extortion/sextortion: ic3.gov
- RAINN online chat for sexual-assault survivors and loved ones: rainn.org/get-help
- Find local services via 211 (dial 2-1-1) in many U.S. counties for crisis resources, shelters, and local referral services.

What to have ready when you call to helps responders act quickly

- Child's name, age, birthdate, address, and school.
- Description of the urgent concern and when it began. Be factual: dates, times, locations, observable behaviors, injuries.
- Name, relationship to the child, and contact information for the suspected abuser (if known).
- Any immediate safety concerns (weapons in the home, threats, medical needs).
- Screenshots, messages, usernames, photos, and device information (preserve evidence —

do NOT alter or delete). Note times, dates, and platforms used.
- Your name and contact information and whether you are a mandated reporter or a relative/caregiver.

Sample reporting script (phone) "I am calling because I have a concern for [child's name], age [x]. I believe [concern—e.g., he/she may be being sexually abused by/trafficked by/receiving explicit images from] [name or online username]. This is what I've observed: [brief facts — dates, times, messages, injuries]. I need guidance on immediate safety steps and how to preserve evidence. What should I do right now?"

Appendix B

National & Local Hotlines and Reporting Resources

Quick overview

Technology can protect or create risk depending on how it's used. Your goals are threefold:

- Reduce exposure to harmful content and contacts.
- Create visibility so dangerous patterns are noticed early.
- Teach children safe habits while preserving opportunities for healthy independence as they mature.

Device-level controls: Built into phones, tablets, and -consoles.

- Set screen limits, app approvals, content ratings, and purchase restrictions. (Apple Screen Time, Google Family Link, Microsoft Family Safety).
- Filtering and DNS services: Block categories of websites at the network level or by DNS. (OpenDNS/CleanBrowsing, router filters.) Good for blocking porn, gambling, or other categories across every device.
- Router-level controls & hardware: Manage access for every device on your network, schedule internet

access, and create guest networks. (Circle Home Plus, router parental-control features).

- Monitoring and alerting services: Scan messages, social media, and searches for risk words/behaviors (grooming, sexting, self-harm). Send alerts to parents. (Bark, Qustodio, Net Nanny, Norton Family).
- Accountability software: Focuses on porn/explicit content—records activity or sends reports to an accountability partner. (Covenant Eyes).
- App blockers & scheduling: Allow parents to block specific apps on schedule or remotely (OurPact, FamilyTime).

Password managers & 2FA tools:

- Keep account credentials secure and enable two-factor authentication to prevent account takeovers. (1Password, LastPass, Bitwarden.)

VPN-awareness & restrictions:

- For older kids, understand and block unauthorized VPNs that can circumvent filters.

Top recommended tools & practices:

- Apple Screen Time (iOS/iPadOS/macOS) — native controls, app limits, content & privacy restrictions, communicate downtime rules. Best for Apple households.
- Google Family Link (Android/Chromebook) — manage apps, set screen time, approve installs for younger accounts. Best for Android/Chromebook.

- Bark — monitors texts, email, YouTube, and 30+ social platforms for grooming, sexting, depression, and self-harm; sends prioritized alerts. Best for broad social monitoring and early warning.
- Covenant Eyes — accountability and filtering focused on pornography; sends activity reports to accountability partners. Best for homes combating porn exposure.
- Net Nanny — content filtering, screen time, app management, and strong web filtering. Good balance of control and usability.
- Qustodio — device management, web filtering, location tracking, and app blocking across platforms. Good for families who want centralized control.
- Circle Home Plus — router-level device management and profiles for each family member; easy scheduling and filtering for all devices on the network. Best for whole-house protection.
- OpenDNS/CleanBrowsing — DNS-level filtering that blocks categories on any device using your network or set per device. Affordable, reliable baseline filter.
- 1Password / Bitwarden — secure password manager for family vaults and shared credentials. Essential for account security.
- Router & network controls (high impact, one-time setup).
- Use router-based filtering (Circle Home Plus or built-in router parental controls) to enforce site categories and schedules across all devices. This blocks many threats before a device sees them.
- Create a guest network for visitors and separate IoT devices- from children's devices.
- Disable UPnP on the router and keep firmware updated.

- Device-level setup basics (first priorities).
- Central charging & no-phones-in-bed rule: Make bedrooms device-free at night.
- Create family accounts: Use Apple Family Sharing or Google Family Link to manage child accounts.
- Enable Screen Time / Family Link: Set daily limits, downtime, app restrictions, and content ratings.
- Approve apps: Require parent approval for new app installs and purchases.
- Turn on location sharing for younger kids (Find My / Family Link) with clear rules.
- Use built-in web filters and disable private / incognito browsing for younger users.
- Set strong device passcodes and enable Find My / remote-wipe options.

Game consoles & streaming devices

- Apply platform parental controls (PlayStation, Xbox, Nintendo Switch) to restrict communication, purchases, and mature content.
- Disable voice/text chat with strangers; restrict play to friends only.
- Lock purchases behind a parent account and use PINs.
- Monitoring services: pros, cons, and how to use them.

Pros: Provide early alerts (grooming language, self-harm signals, sexting), scan many platforms, and can catch patterns you might miss.

Cons: False positives, privacy concerns, and can create trust issues if used secretly. They are not a substitute for conversation.

Best use: Be transparent—tell children monitoring is in place for safety. Use alerts as reasons to have calm conversations, not immediate punishments. Have a plan for each alert: check safety, preserve evidence if needed, and escalate to professionals when appropriate.

Age-based recommended stacks (practical starting points).

Young children (0–8): Router-level filtering + device in parent control, screen-free bedrooms, no social accounts, supervised content (YouTube Kids), strict app approvals.

Tweens (9–12): Family Link / Screen Time + Bark or Net Nanny for monitoring + DNS filtering + central charging + weekly check-in drills. Covenant Eyes for inappropriate images.

Early teens (13–15): Net Nanny or Qustodio + Bark for social monitoring + negotiated social accounts with clear rules + monthly tech-summits. Covenant Eyes for inappropriate images.

Older teens (16+): Transition to negotiated privacy: teach account security, require a password manager, keep device visibility (location) and device-free times, use monitoring only for high-risk situations. Covenant Eyes for inappropriate image monitoring and Bark for texting accountability. Consider gradual reduction of intrusive monitoring as trust and responsibility are proven.

Practical setup checklist (step-by-step)

- Inventory every device in your home (phones, tablets, laptops, consoles, smart speakers).

- Set a central family email/identity for account recovery and admin control.
- Create or convert child accounts to managed family accounts (Apple/Google).
- Enable Screen Time or Family Link and set base rules (bedtime, no social before X age, app approvals).
- Install a monitoring service (Bark/Net Nanny/Qustodio) and configure alert thresholds.
- Set up router-level filtering or Circle Home Plus and create profiles for each child.
- Turn on two-factor authentication for all major accounts (parents and children where age-appropriate).
- Set up a password manager with a family vault and teach basic password hygiene.
- Place emergency tech rules and scripts in the family safety binder and teach one caregiver tonight how to respond to alerts.

Run a 5-minute drill: use the family code word, simulate an alert, and practice the first response steps.

Best practices & family policies (non-technical)

- **Be transparent:** Tell children what is monitored and why. Transparency preserves trust and increases the chance they will come to you when something goes wrong.
- **Negotiate rules with older kids:** Give growing autonomy in exchange for accountability (e.g., location sharing for late nights).
- **Make device-free routines sacred**: Mealtimes, bedtime, and family time without screens. No phones in bedroom or bathroom.

- **Teach evidence steps:** If a child reports sextortion or grooming, preserve messages/screenshots and do not confront the suspect.
- **Periodic reviews**: Monthly family tech meetings to review apps, settings, and any alerts.
- **Responding to an alert**: immediate parent actions.
- **Assess safety:** Is the child in immediate danger? If yes, call 911.
- **Preserve evidence:** Screenshot messages, save URLs, back up chats. Do not alter original devices if forensic evidence may be needed.
- **Ask calmly and listen:** Use non-judgmental language to let the child tell you what happened.
- **Escalate:** If abuse, trafficking, or criminal behavior is suspected, call local police and the appropriate hotline (NCMEC, Human Trafficking Hotline).
- **Get help:** Contact a child-advocacy center, a SANE nurse for forensic exams if applicable, and a trauma-informed counselor.

Privacy, consent, and legal notes

- Laws differ by jurisdiction; parents who are also mandated reporters (teachers, medical professionals) have separate obligations. Check local laws.
- Monitoring can have unintended consequences—use it as a safety tool, not as covert punishment. Consider the child's age and mental health when choosing intensity of monitoring.
- If monitoring an older teen, discuss boundaries and consider a gradual, agreed-upon reduction of monitoring as trust is earned.

Avoiding common pitfalls

- Don't rely solely on tech: filters can be bypassed, and algorithms miss grooming nuance. Adult supervision and conversations are primary protection.
- Don't use monitoring to snoop for discipline reasons only; that undermines the relationship and encourages secrecy.
- Don't ignore alerts: a flagged message may be a false positive, but it may also be the first chance to stop harm.

Resources & where to learn more

- Apple: Screen Time and Family Sharing support pages.
- Google: Family Link help center.
- Bark (bark.us) — product guides and platform list.
- Covenant Eyes (covenanteyes.com) — accountability and filtering resources.
- Net Nanny (netnanny.com), Qustodio (qustodio.com), Norton Family (us.norton.com/family).
- Circle Home Plus (meetcircle.com) and OpenDNS (opendns.com) / CleanBrowsing (cleanbrowsing.org).

Final note: Tech is a powerful ally when paired with clear language, practiced responses, and adult presence. Start with the basics tonight: central charging, a family password manager, Screen Time/Family Link, and at least one monitoring or router-level filter. Teach one caregiver the emergency scripts and put those pages where you can reach them immediately. Then iterate—small steps, practiced until they are muscle memory, will multiply into real safety.

Appendix C

Legal Basics – Mandatory Reporting & What to Expect

This appendix explains the practical legal steps when you suspect a child is being harmed. It is written for clarity and action, not as legal advice. Laws vary by state and role—when in doubt, report immediately and consult local counsel or a child-welfare advocate for case-specific guidance.

Why this matters

Reporting suspected abuse, neglect, exploitation, or trafficking is not optional for many professionals and is often the fastest way to get a child out of danger. Timely reporting preserves evidence, triggers protective services, and connects families to medical and trauma-informed help.

Who is a mandated reporter

Mandated reporters are people required by law to report suspected child abuse or neglect. Typical categories include:

- Teachers, school staff, and coaches.
- Medical professionals, nurses, and hospital staff (including SANE nurses).
- Mental-health professionals and counselors.
- Child-care providers and foster-care workers.
- Social workers and law-enforcement officers.

- Clergy in some states (check local rules).
- Other professionals who regularly work with children (varies by state).
- If you are unsure whether you are a mandated reporter, assume you should report—or call your state's child-protective services (CPS) for guidance.

What must be reported

Report if you have a reasonable suspicion that a child:

- Has been abused or neglected (physical, sexual, emotional).
- Is being sexually exploited, trafficked, or coerced.
- Is at imminent risk of harm (threats, weapons, suicidal intent).
- Has unexplained serious injuries or behaviors indicating abuse.
- "Reasonable suspicion" is a low legal threshold—you do not need proof. If something feels wrong, report it.

When to report

- Immediate danger or medical emergency: call 911 now.
- Non-immediate but urgent concerns: call your local CPS hotline or law-enforcement non-emergency number the same day. Many jurisdictions require reports "immediately" or "within 24 hours." Do not delay to gather proof.

How to make a report

- Call the local CPS / child protective services hotline for your county or state. (If you don't know the number, call local police non-emergency or 2-1-1).
- If a crime may have occurred, notify law enforcement as well. CPS and law enforcement often coordinate.
- Many agencies accept online reports; use them if available and appropriate.
- If you are a mandated reporter, follow your employer's reporting protocols after making the required external report.

What to have ready when you call (brief checklist)

- Child's name, age, birthdate, address, school.
- Your name, relationship to child, and contact info (you can request confidentiality in some cases).
- Concise facts: what you observed, dates/times, exact words the child used (use their words in quotes), injuries, and who else knows.
- Name and relationship of suspected abuser (if known). Any immediate safety risks (weapons, threats).
- Any physical evidence (screenshots, photos, clothing)—note where it is stored.

A short reporting script (use or adapt)

"I'm calling to report a concern for [child's name], age [x]. I have reason to believe [brief description: e.g., they may have been sexually abused by/are being trafficked by/are receiving explicit images from] [name or username]. Here's what I observed: [concise facts—dates, times, messages, injuries]. What immediate steps should I take to keep this child safe?"

What happens after you report

Procedures vary, but common steps include:

- Screening/triage: CPS decides whether the report meets the threshold for investigation.
- Investigation or assessment: CPS, often with law enforcement, will gather information, interview adults, and arrange a forensic interview for the child (conducted by trained interviewers).
- Safety planning: If the child is unsafe, CPS may implement a safety plan—temporary removal, supervised visits, or emergency placement.
- Medical evaluation: For sexual abuse or assault concerns, a SANE (Sexual Assault Nurse Examiner) or child-friendly medical exam may be arranged.
- Referral to services: Counseling, advocacy, shelter, or trafficking survivor services.
- Possible criminal investigation: Law enforcement may investigate in parallel; prosecutors decide on charges.

Your role as the reporter

- Provide factual information, not conclusions. Use objective language and the child's own words.
- Preserve evidence (screenshots, messages, clothing) and document contemporaneous notes—date, time, who said what, who was present. Keep originals secure.
- Do not repeatedly interview the child—leave forensic interviewing to trained professionals.

- Cooperate with investigators and advocates. Answer follow-up questions promptly.
- Maintain confidentiality as advised by CPS or legal counsel.

Confidentiality and reporter protections

- Many states protect reporters with immunity from civil or criminal liability when reports are made in good faith.
- Some hotlines allow anonymous reporting; mandated reporters may still be required to identify themselves depending on state law.
- If you fear retaliation (workplace, family), inform the agency and document concerns. Seek legal advice if needed.

If you disagree with the agency response

- Ask to speak to a supervisor at CPS or law enforcement for clarification.
- Request that your report be escalated or re-reviewed if new information emerges.
- Contact your local child advocacy center or a victim advocate for guidance and support.
- In persistent inaction, you may contact the state child-welfare ombudsman or consult an attorney.

Criminal vs. civil processes — two separate tracks

- Criminal: law enforcement investigates; prosecutors decide on charges; criminal trials require proof beyond a reasonable doubt.
- Civil/child-welfare: CPS focuses on child safety and family services; the standard is often "preponderance

of evidence." CPS can remove a child or require services even if no criminal charges are filed.
- Both tracks can proceed concurrently.

Forensic interviews and medical exams

- Forensic interviews are conducted by trained professionals in child-friendly settings (often at child advocacy centers) to reduce retraumatization and preserve evidence for court.
- SANE/pediatric forensic exams provide medical care, STI testing, emergency contraception if needed, and evidence collection. A medical exam can occur without pressing criminal charges.
- Avoid repeating the child's account; refer them to the forensic interviewer.

Working with schools, churches, and organizations

- Organizations should have written reporting policies and a designated person to contact CPS. Staff who are mandated reporters must report directly even if an internal report is made.
- Do not rely on an institution to "handle internally." Reporting to CPS or law enforcement is required in many cases and is appropriate for safety and evidence reasons.

If the suspected abuser is a family member or caregiver

- Safety planning is urgent. If immediate danger exists, call 911.
- CPS may remove the child or the alleged abuser pending investigation.

- Avoid confronting the accused—doing so can increase risk and interfere with investigations.

Cross-jurisdictional and international issues

- If the suspected abuse crosses state or national lines (online predators, trafficking), report to local law enforcement and national hotlines (see Appendix A). Federal agencies (FBI) may become involved.
- International cases may require coordination with foreign authorities—consult law enforcement and trafficking hotlines for guidance.

Documentation checklist (what to save)

- Exact quotes and disclosures (child's words, in quotes). Dates/times/locations of incidents and observations.
- Photos of injuries, saved messages, screenshots (include timestamps and usernames).
- Names of witnesses and their contact info.
- Copies of reports you made (CPS reference number, officer name, date/time of call).

Practical tips for parents and caregivers

- Prioritize safety: if unsafe, remove the child to a safe place and call 911.
- Preserve evidence and document.
- Seek medical attention when needed and ask for a SANE/forensic exam if sexual abuse is suspected.
- Contact a child advocacy center or victim advocate to navigate reporting and care.
- Get legal advice if you face custody, protection-order, or complex family-law issues.

Resources and advocacy

- Child advocacy centers, victim advocates, and hotlines offer immediate help, court accompaniment, and service referrals—call a national hotline (Appendix A) if you need local referrals.
- If you are a mandated reporter, use your employer's training, supervision, and reporting protocols—ask for written confirmation when you file a report.

Final reminders

- Reasonable suspicion—not proof—is the legal trigger for reporting. You are not responsible for proving abuse; you are responsible for reporting concerns so professionals can investigate.
- Do not confront suspected abusers. Preserve evidence. Cooperate with investigators. Seek professional support for yourself and the child.
- When in doubt, report. The cost of failing to act can be catastrophic.
- If you need a local number or immediate guidance, call any national hotline listed in Appendix A — they will connect you with local resources and next steps.

Acknowledgements

This book grew out of pain, witness, and relentless work. I am deeply grateful to the children and survivors who trusted me with pieces of their stories—your courage and honesty are the reason these pages exist.

Thank you to the detectives, prosecutors, SANE nurses, advocates, therapists, social-service professionals, and researchers who shared time, expertise, and hard data. Your guidance turned raw experience into responsible, practical steps. Thank you to the staff at child-advocacy centers, hotlines, and survivor organizations who do the daily, often invisible work of rescue and healing.

To the churches, schools, coaches, and program leaders who opened policies and spaces to scrutiny: your willingness to change keeps children safer. To foster and adoptive families, volunteers, and caregivers who show up every day—your steady presence matters more than words can say.

To the editors, designers, legal reviewers, and clinicians who read drafts, corrected me, and insisted on clarity and care—this book is better because of you.

To Mandy Draganic, thank you for the long phone calls while editing and for being my grammar police.

And to the reader: thank you for taking this work seriously. You'll find repetition here on purpose—practice turns knowledge into action when it counts. Teach one person what you learn, place the emergency pages where you can reach them, and act. If these pages help even one child, every hard hour that birthed them will have been worth it.

If you found A Predator Within useful, I would really appreciate a short review. Your help in spreading the word is highly valued and reviews make it much easier for readers to find the book.

PAINFULLY BROKEN

Yet Beautifully Redeemed

ANGELA RODGERS

FROM
DARKNESS
TO LIGHT

ANGELA RODGERS

www.ingramcontent.com/pod-product-compliance
Lightning Source LLC
Chambersburg PA
CBHW070913130626
46555CB00001B/108